W9-CIM-851

Understanding Children & Youth with Emotional & Behavioral Problems

A Handbook for Parents & Professionals

Paul Zionts
Central Michigan University

Richard L. Simpson
University of Kansas

5341 Industrial Oaks Boulevard
Austin, Texas 78735

123500

Copyright © 1988 by PRO-ED, Inc.

All rights reserved. No part of this book
may be reproduced in any form or by any means
without the prior written permission of the publisher.

Printed in the United States of America

Library of Congress Cataloging-in-Publication Data

Zionts, Paul., 1950–
   Understanding children and youth with emotional and
behavioral problems: a handbook for parents and professionals
/ Paul Zionts, Richard L. Simpson.
      p.   cm.
   ISBN 0-89079-170-8
   1. Problem children—Handbooks, manuals, etc. 2. Emotional problems of children—Handbooks, manuals, etc.
3. Problem children—Services for—United States—Directories.
I. Simpson, Richard L., 1945–   . II. Title.
HQ773.Z47 1988
362.2'088054—dc19   87-29798

5341 Industrial Oaks Boulevard
Austin, Texas 78735

10 9 8 7 6 5 4 3 2 1   88 89 90 91 92

Contents

123⁵00

Preface

Conservative estimates from both educators and mental health professionals indicate that approximately 10% of children and adolescents in this country will experience emotional and behavioral problems serious enough to require professional attention. In addition, a sizeable percentage of children and youth can be expected periodically to encounter social and other adjustment difficulties. Based on these statistics, children and adolescents with emotional and behavioral conflicts are a reality for many families who must learn to cope with the day-to-day challenges of meeting the special needs of their troubled youngster.

Understanding Children and Youth with Emotional and Behavioral Problems: A Handbook for Parents and Professionals is designed to be a resource for persons dealing with children and adolescents who evidence emotional and behavioral disabilities. In spite of the great number of young people who experience behavioral and emotional problems, limited lay information is available on the topic. In addition, professionals also report a paucity of basic information about childhood emotional problems. As a result, both lay persons (including parents and family members) and professionals are often left groping for answers to questions about children's and adolescents' behavioral and emotional problems, including definitions, causes, treatment methods, and support services. This book will prove helpful to both of these reader groups. Specifically, parents and families will find it useful as they attempt to understand their children and the services available to meet their needs. Similarly, professionals having contact with emotionally disturbed and behavior-problem children and youth will gain a better understanding of these youngsters. Thus, the book is of particular value to physicians, nurses, social workers, judges, juvenile workers, occupational therapists, physical therapists, speech pathologists, teachers, counselors, and a myriad of other professionals who have periodic contact with problem children and youth.

The book is designed to provide straightforward, basic information about childhood and adolescent emotional and behavior problems. Using a question-answer format, practical questions are posed and followed by easy-to-follow, functional responses. The book is composed of eight major sections: (a) definition and conceptualization of the emotional and behavioral problems of children and youth; (b) causes; (c) identification and assessment methods; (d) major forms of emotional and behavioral problems; (e) sources of assistance; (f) treatment methods; (g) parent and family involvement; and (h) the future. A glossary of terms and a list of organizations serving parents and professionals working with children and adolescents with behavior and emotional disabilities are also included.

Introduction to Emotional Disturbance and Behavioral Disorders

 Phone calls from school . . . disapproving looks from relatives and friends . . . difficulty finding someone for her to play with . . . always seems to be in "trouble" . . . or perhaps, is frequently alone, both on the playground and at home . . . rarely talks or plays with brothers and sisters. People are concerned. Yet, what can be done? What do we know? What do we need to know?

Is my child emotionally disturbed?

The reason you are reading this book is that you either suspect or have already been told that your child (or one that you know or are working with) may be emotionally disturbed or behaviorally disordered. Certainly, many questions and issues have crossed your mind. Does this mean that the child is "crazy"? Will the child have to undergo therapy for hours? Days? Years? Will the child have to be hospitalized? Does this mean medication? What can be done? What does "emotional disturbance" mean?

One of the most confusing and potentially explosive labels that can be attached to a child (and, perhaps, family) is *emotional disturbance*. Its exact impact on the family can only be speculated. A variety of reactions may occur. Compounding the potential family impact is the possible feeling of shame at having a child with emotional or behavioral problems. What do you tell your relatives and friends? You may find that everyone seems to be an expert on this subject.

The purpose of this chapter is to answer some of the initial questions that cross the minds of parents and others who live or work with emotionally disturbed or behaviorally disordered children and youth. Virtually all the topics in this chapter will be discussed in more depth throughout the book.

Is it my fault?

This is probably the single most asked question. It is also a question that has no clearcut answer, except that, in most cases, it is not the parents' fault that a child is having emotional or behavioral problems.

There is little evidence to suggest that any one person or incident can be blamed. Clearly, the child is behaving in a manner which warrants some attention, yet. . . ? These feelings and questions are normal and are experienced by many parents. Exploring and understanding these reactions is extremely important and may help both the reader and the child avoid secondary problems.

Is it my child's fault? He's smart enough to behave better!

Again, a focus on blame will rarely help anybody and, in many cases, hinders the child's progress. But, the second part of this question (i.e., He's smart enough to behave better.) raises a very important point. Intelligence has little to do with the occurrence of emotional problems. While it is natural to be frustrated when a smart child seemingly should "know better," being smart doesn't necessarily mean that one is emotionally healthy. Many intelligent people have emotional problems.

How many children are emotionally disturbed?

Incidence, or the number of children and adolescents identified as having emotional disturbance or behavioral disorders, is the source of major controversy among professionals. As there is a confusion regarding the definition of the problem itself, it follows that the percentage of children who are labeled emotionally disturbed will vary according to the group or individual doing the labeling. Except in the most severe cases, it is extremely difficult to arrive at an exact number of children with emotional disturbance. The United States Office of Education has estimated that 2% of the kindergarten through 12-grade student population are seriously emotionally disturbed. As will be discussed later, most people have different ideas about the definition of emotional disturbance. Consequently, the number of children so identified varies. Also, there may be other factors that enable or hinder identification of these children and youth.

Various groups have estimated percentages of behaviorally disordered and emotionally disturbed children ranging from 1% to 40% of the school-aged population. In comparison, public school administrators believe that the number of children and youth so classified should be 2%, while teachers have contended that between 10% and 40% of their students have problems severe enough to warrant professional attention.

This confusion is compounded by the fact that some students who exhibit maladaptive or "problem" behaviors at school do not exhibit them at home. Further, it is often difficult to determine if a child's problems are going to be short-lived (growing pains) or if they will drastically affect the long-term emotional growth of the child.

To determine if a child's problems are, in fact, "growing pains," you must understand how other children of similar ages behave and express their emotions. By definition, a child is an individual who is not fully developed: cognitively, physically, socially, and emotionally. Therefore, it is important to be aware of behaviors that are common to particular age groups. One study suggested that one-third to one-half of 8-year-olds may be identified as overactive and restless. Again, it is when the child is significantly different from peers that concern should arise.

This section has not yet described those children and adolescents who are frequently labeled as severely emotionally disturbed or autistic. The onset of autism usually takes place before 2 years of age. Further, autism is relatively rare (approximately .05%). Earlier it was suggested that disturbing behaviors may be a result of the tolerance of those observing the child. This is not the case with autism. To most observers autistic behaviors are clearly abnormal.

How much of this information should we share with our child?

A very important point to consider is the child's feelings and perspective. Does he even perceive the behavior(s) that are so upsetting to others? The more involved children are in the various interactions and meetings that take place regarding their problems, the more committed they may be to participate in remediation attempts.

Talking with children can sometimes shed light on matters that have been incorrectly perceived or interpreted by others. A knowledge of what your child can handle and consultation with school or counseling personnel can best answer this question.

How will my child be treated at school?

This depends upon the type of emotional disturbance or behavioral disorder the child has. If children are demonstrating negative attention-getting behaviors, they are likely receiving negative feedback from their parents, their teachers, and, possibly, their friends.

It doesn't necessarily follow that others will view a child's problems as "new" once they have been identified. If the diagnosis leads to a new educational placement for the child, it may become necessary to help the child cope with the new setting.

Emotional disturbance or behavioral disorders: What's the difference?

Much of the time, the only difference is the label. It might be helpful to distinguish between two types of labels: *Official labels*, which are used on official documents and heard in such formal environments as school and clinics, and *informal labels*, which may occur in private or maybe only in one's thoughts!

What are official labels?

Before we discuss the labels, we must remember that there is also a controversy regarding the diagnosis (how one is identified and labeled) of emotional disturbance. At least three different views of cause exist. Some diagnosticians may have only one view of disturbance and, thus, may ignore the other possibilities. Further, test results may be less valid *due to the child's behaviors* during the testing situation. For example, the child may behave in such an erratic manner that an accurate evaluation may be difficult to obtain. Such behavior might be due to emotional disturbance *or* something as "normal" as acting different because of nervousness about the testing. Finally, it is difficult to pinpoint a specific cause, or two or more causes, interacting together.

Most often, the first official label is given to a disturbed child in school. Labels for a child's behavior may vary vastly depending upon the state of residence. Frequently used labels include *emotionally disturbed, emotionally impaired, behaviorally disordered, conduct disordered, socially maladjusted,* or the more general, *educationally handicapped.*

It is important to understand that these labels usually have virtually the same meaning to educators and parents. That is, they are used to identify and describe students who are socially, behaviorally or emotionally different from their peers. Much time and energy has been spent on determining the most appropriate label. The authors believe that it is the manner in which labels are used that should be the major concern (such as avoiding them in the presence of the children), and *not* the labels themselves.

In other words, it is the manner of treatment that should receive the greatest priority.

For children and youth who exhibit extremely different (or deviant) behaviors, the word *severely* may be attached to their label, such as *severely emotionally disturbed.* Another term for this population is *autistic* or *autistic-like*, although states have placed autistic individuals in a separate category. Severely emotionally disturbed students most often cannot handle the rigors of a regular classroom setting, requiring instead a specialized classroom in a public school or a residential setting.

Regardless of the label, it is important to remember that the focus should be on the child. These children are *probably* more similar to "normal" than not! They have good days and "bad" days. Usually they have more bad periods during the day or more bad days compared to their peers. Nevertheless, we should avoid the temptation to consider the emotionally disturbed child as *always* being bad.

What are informal labels?

Unfortunately, informal labels are probably more of a problem to children and youth than formal labels. Informal labels are automatically attached to a person's behavior when that behavior is very different from what is expected. People may label either the behavior or the person as "weird." This is when problems may surface. Some individuals tend to label a person's *essence* rather than label a particular behavior, especially when the behavior is unusual in a negative way. In other words, if someone does something that is not normally accepted, he or she might be thought of as being a "crazy" person.

Clearly, we cannot control the thoughts of others, and individuals *do* have different standards of behaviors. It is when children are discriminated against, both overtly and covertly, that their emotional health may be in danger. This is not to suggest that we should allow children to run rampant through our homes and schools without attempting to bring about behavioral changes. Rather, behaviors should be dealt with and, in the process, we must avoid condemnation of the child.

How States View Labels

Regardless of the specific label a state has designated for students with emotional disturbance and behavioral problems, most refer to the population that is addressed in this book.

How Researchers View Labels

While the preceding information holds true for the way most practitioners view emotional disturbance and behavioral disorders, some researchers believe that the label gives some very specific information about the etiology or the *cause* of an individual's problems. They believe that when students are labeled emotionally disturbed, they have deep-rooted psychological problems that call for an intervention program of psychotherapy. If students are labeled "behaviorally disordered," their problem is observable, it is more easily identified, and an intervention program can be more readily designed and implemented by teachers and parents.

How are people labeled "emotionally disturbed" or "behaviorally disordered"?

Three factors are often considered when determining if a child is disturbed: intensity, pattern, and duration of behavior. *Intensity* refers to the severity of the child's problem. How does it get in the way of the child's (or society's) goals? How much does it draw attention from others? For obvious reasons, this factor is the easiest to identify.

Pattern refers to the times when the problems occur. Do problems only occur during the school day? Only during math class? At bedtime? Answers to these questions may yield very helpful diagnostic and remediation information.

Finally, *duration* refers to the length of time the child's problem has been present. For example, some school districts require a 3-month period before they suggest that a child has an emotional or behavioral problem.

How can I make practical sense of these three factors?

Bower (1959) proposed a developmental continuum for identifying emotional disturbance in children and youth. At this point, it will serve as a useful reference point for the reader:

Stage 1. Children who experience and demonstrate the normal problems of everyday living, growing, exploration, and reality testing.

Stage 2. Children who develop a greater number and degree of symptoms of emotional problems as a result of a crisis or traumatic experience.

Stage 3. Children in whom symptoms persist to some extent beyond normal expectation but who can adjust adequately to school.

Stage 4. Children with fixed and recurring symptoms of emotional disturbance, who can, with help, maintain some positive relationships in a school setting.

Stage 5. Children with fixed and recurring symptoms of emotional difficulties who are best educated in a residential school setting or temporarily in a home setting.

Clearly, by referring to the five stages, almost any child who is different from what is considered normal may be labeled disturbed. A closer look at these stages suggests that according to Stage 1, most children exhibit disturbing behaviors sometime in their lives. Thus, concerned parties should be careful not to overreact to an isolated disturbing event in a child's life.

What kinds of behaviors fit into these educational stages?

Bower[1] suggested several general behaviors that may be included in a definition of emotional disturbance. According to Bower,

---

[1]Bower, C. M. (1959). The emotionally handicapped and the school. *Exceptional Children, 26,* 6–11.

emotionally disturbed children are those who demonstrate one or more of the following characteristics to a *marked extent* (intensity) and *over a period of time* (pattern):

1. An inability to learn which cannot be explained by intellectual, sensory or health factors.

2. An inability to build or maintain satisfactory interpersonal relationships with peers or teachers.

3. Inappropriate types of behaviors or feelings under normal conditions.

4. A general, pervasive mood of unhappiness or depression.

5. A tendency to develop physical symptoms, pains, or fears associated with personal or school problems.

These descriptions obviously are educational in nature. Yet, with generalizations to both home and community, the definition can serve as a useful reference.

The most important message in this context is that the term *emotional disturbance* (or *behavioral disorder, social maladjustment, emotional handicap*, etc.) is extremely general and ambiguous. It can mean a variety of things to different people. Many research studies have found that the term has different meanings for parents, teachers, counselors, principals, doctors, and even the child's friends. The following two vignettes illustrate how difficult it is to identify and understand emotional disturbance and behavioral disorders:

Sally and Joe

SALLY has been a very pleasant student in her 5-grade classroom all year. She is attractive, well-mannered, and does well in school. She sits in the front row and appropriately smiles, answers questions, and participates in group discussions. She is an only child and her parents have traditionally taken an active interest in her school progress. She is extremely close to her mother.

Tragically, her mother is in a car accident and subsequently dies. Sally becomes sullen and withdrawn. Her father leaves her alone believing she is undergoing a normal grieving period. However, 10 days pass and Sally's withdrawn behavior continues. Her father decides that it would be best for her to return to school to help her come out of the depression.

Upon Sally's return she quietly moves her seat to the back of the classroom. The teacher tries gently to persuade Sally to participate, but also understands what Sally must be going through and decides to leave her alone. When the teacher has time she attempts to counsel Sally. However, no matter what she does to help her, Sally's withdrawn behavior continues. After a meeting with other school professionals it was decided to let Sally stay in class in the hope that, with time, she will return to her "normal" self.

JOE has been a pain-in-the-neck to almost everybody he has been in contact with this year. He is unkempt, ill mannered, and a C–D (below average) student. Joe's teacher seems to always be calling out his name for classroom infractions. While his mother was initially responsive to contacts from the school, she has recently stopped her attempts to cooperate. She has admitted to the principal that she was at the "end of her rope" with Joe at home. Joe's father, while professing concern, works long hours in his new business, and is generally uninvolved with his son.

One day, Joe's mother dies. During the next week, Joe, who had been extremely close to his mother, engages in many tantrums. His father lets him alone believing that this is the normal grieving period. While taking the week off from work, his father found it very difficult to communicate with Joe. Finally, he decided that Joe should return to school.

Upon Joe's return, he storms into the classroom kicking chairs and throwing papers all over the room. He runs to his desk screaming, "I hate her! I hate her! She left me, the bitch! I hate her, I hate her, I hate her!" The teacher tries to quiet Joe with no success. After a meeting with other school professionals it was decided that Joe might need special help.

Joe and Sally represent students who may be equally *disturbed*. Yet, their behaviors demonstrate that the nature of their disturbances is different, that is, Joe was disturbing and Sally was withdrawn. Consequently, society's reactions to Joe and Sally are different. While both examples focus upon the death of a mother and its effects on children, rarely will the children's reactions be as strong as those portrayed here. Nevertheless, in most instances somebody like Sally will be allowed to continue to act disturbed in her quiet, withdrawn manner. Students like Joe, on the other hand, will most likely be removed from the regular class and treatment may be deemed necessary.

Some people believe that it is only those children who are *disturbing*, such as Joe, who are regularly identified as emotionally disturbed. Withdrawn students, such as Sally, are often more difficult to identify, and, ultimately, help.

Normally, children are diagnosed as disturbed when their behavior is very different from that of their peers and/or what is expected of them. The problem behaviors may only be recent or they may be long-term. The disturbances may be demonstrated in the classroom, where such abstract assignments as reading and writing are required, or only in the home, where tasks tend to be more concrete, such as taking out the garbage, washing dishes, or mowing the lawn.

Refer again to the three factors that generally determine assignment of a label. Both Sally and Joe seem to belong in Bower's (1959) Stage 2. That is, their feelings and behaviors seem to be a result of a one-time traumatic experience. Yet, the action parents and concerned professionals take may have an influence on either child's future emotional growth.

What are the possible causes of emotional disturbance and behavioral disorders?

There is rarely a simple cause of emotional disturbance. Diagnosis may occur almost any time in an individual's life, as emotional problems can surface at any age. In fact, it is common for all of us to be occasionally emotionally disturbed, as evidenced in severe anger, depression, or extreme frustration.

Complex factors, such as a student's environment, a deep-rooted psychological problem, or a biophysical imbalance may each contribute to different feelings and/or behavioral problems. Further, there may be several factors interacting with one another.

Briefly, when the *environment* is considered to be a major contributor to students' problems, many questions are explored: What is happening at home?; is the home culturally different from the school resulting in behaviors being accepted at home and not at school?; are the economic conditions at home significantly less favorable than those of others preventing equal participation in school activities (play pay sports, etc.)?; and do the significant people (teachers, community, relatives) in children's lives hold differential expectations? In other words, identification of disturbing behaviors may be a result of the degree of flexibility and tolerance the concerned members of the child's environment demonstrate.

Deep-rooted psychological problems involve uneven or deficient personality development as reflected in pathological (repeated, long term) behaviors. Traditionally, most behavior problems have been perceived as the result of a disturbed psyche. The common psychological term for these behavioral problems is *phobias*. Phobias are fears and anxieties that prevent people from behaving "normally" or appropriately in everyday situations. Like other types of disturbances, phobia may be temporary or long term.

In the 1950s, '60s, and '70s, much of the thought and practice in school psychology was heavily influenced by psychological theory. In recent years, the psychological theory of disturbance has become less popular, especially when school-based disturbances are considered. This is primarily due to the rather inefficient process (it takes a long time before results are apparent) that is normally associated with the psychological approach. Most teachers believe that they don't have the time and, perhaps, expertise to effectively utilize the needed counseling techniques. Nevertheless, community-based mental health agencies may utilize this approach.

A *biophysical imbalance* or medical problem implies that the students' problems are largely internal. That is, the students cannot change the behaviors at will. Many theories suggest that prenatal (before birth) or perinatal (after birth) illnesses, unusually long childbirth, heredity, and/or inappropriate levels of certain body chemicals may contribute to or cause emotional disorders.

As with the other areas of disturbance, much controversy and debate surround these theories as direct links to specific emotional or behavioral disturbance.

A more severe example of possible biophysical imbalances are individuals with schizophrenia, autism, or autistic-like behaviors. Such children represent a particular challenge to both parents and professionals as they are integrated less successfully in either public schools or the community due to highly noticeable differences in their thinking, social, and speech and language skills.

Occasionally, one of the above theories is the predominant factor in determining a possible cause. However, each factor has many dimensions, several of which will be discussed in Chapters 2 and 3 along with specific interventions.

Whatever the cause or label, it is important that the involved parties understand the exact nature of the problem. What is meant by a given label *in this case*? What is the child doing to be labeled and, more importantly, what *can* the child do and what are some realistic behavioral expectations? When unclear about the manner in which the term *emotional disturbance* is being used, ask for clarification, especially if causation is implied. Concerned individuals have the right to know as much as possible. A more detailed discussion of causation or etiology will follow in Chapter 3.

What are the characteristics of emotionally disturbed or behaviorally disordered children and youth?

Characteristics of a disturbed child are best described in behavioral terms. That is, rather than talking about a child as "crazy" or "acting-out," a more detailed explanation of specific behaviors and emotions allows all concerned parties to approach the problem with an equal understanding. General categories such as *hyperactive* and *withdrawn* may be good starting points, but give little useful information.

The following behavioral characteristics are intended to explain some of the vague categories that are often used to describe emotional disturbance and behavior disorders. The reader is cautioned not to make hasty generalizations based on familiar behaviors in the categories. In other words, if an acquaintance exhibits two or three of these behaviors, it probably does not mean that the person has a major (pathological) problem. As discussed, factors such as the strength of the emotion and the length of time it is exhibited must be considered when making an appropriate professional diagnosis.

CONDUCT DISORDERS
Fights, hits others
Destroys property
Commits crimes against society
Easily frustrated
Steals
Undependable
Boisterous
Truant
Runs away from home
Persistently lying
Substance abuser
Engages in inappropriate sexual activity
Blames others

ATTENTION AND CONCENTRATION
Can't sit still
Highly distracted by everything
Involved in excessive daydreaming
Doesn't complete chores, assignments
Has poor memory
Has short attention span—maybe as short as
   20 seconds
Doesn't seem to listen
Drowsy
Shows lack of interest

HYPERACTIVITY/ATTENTION DEFICIT
Can't sit still, fidgets
Rushes work

Seems to be talking all the time
May have nervous mannerisms such as twitches
Constantly seeks attention of others
Demonstrates poor organizational skills
Shows lack of goals, direction
Has short attention span
Can't ignore environmental influences
Impulsive
Excessively climbs on things
Needs consistent supervision
Interrupts others
Has frequent temper tantrums

WITHDRAWAL
Seems tired
Avoids interaction with others
Demonstrates lack of interest
Depressed, sad
Passive
Easily embarrassed
Rarely expresses emotions
Doesn't have self-confidence
Feels inferior to others
Shy, timid, fearful

FUNCTION DISORDERS
Eating disorders
    Voluntary regurgitation
    Obesity
    Eating inedible objects (habitually)
    Refusal to eat
Elimination disorders
    Inability to control bladder (no physical reasons)
    Inability to control bowel (no physical reasons)

PSYCHOSES
Autism
    Demonstrates unusual communication patterns
    Has poor language
    Rocks head or body

Flaps arms or hands
Preoccupied with minor visual details
Stares into space
Ignores or doesn't respond to stimuli
Agitated by loud noises
Engages in self-injurious behavior
Masturbates in public
Schizophrenia
Illogical thinking
Delusions
Hallucinations
Disjunctive talking
Unusual perceptions
Self-injurious behavior

The purpose of listing these categories is to give the reader a glossary of behaviors that are often attached to these general and sometimes vague descriptions. The reader must resist the temptation to become an armchair psychologist. Instead, the reader is encouraged to ask the diagnostician about the specific characteristics the child is exhibiting when he or she is "hyperactive."

A rule of thumb is to decide if the above behaviors are deviant enough to call attention to at least one other person or to themselves and/or others. Listing these behaviors may aid the reader in noticing potential signs of trouble. Generally, the reader should begin to be concerned if changes occur in the child's behavioral pattern.

Summary

The purpose of this chapter was to introduce the reader to a general overview of emotional disturbance and behavioral disorders. Each of the topics discussed will be explored in greater depth in other sections of this book. General issues and questions about the topics were raised so that the reader might critically examine the everyday problems of working and living with emotionally disturbed and behaviorally disordered youth.

Various theories of causation (etiology) may be useful when trying to understand the child, but it is important to remember that it is extremely difficult to pinpoint any one reason for the child's behaviors. Further, the central purpose of determining causation or, for that matter, any diagnosis, is to generate interventions. To merely know why something happens has little utility.

A strong message has been delivered in this chapter. *Emotional disturbance* and *behavioral disorders* mean different things to different people. Parents, friends of the family, neighbors, teachers, school administrators, shopkeepers, and doctors may each have their own "expert" opinions. Therefore, communication about the child's *individual* problem must occur. Most often, it will be the reader's responsibility to insist upon getting a clear, understandable message from those concerned. This book should aid the reader in that regard.

What About Cause?

An initial reaction of parents, teachers, relatives, and friends of children experiencing problems is to look for a cause. It is only natural to want to know *why!* Parents of a young hard-of-hearing boy indicated they were distressed to learn their son had a hearing problem but relieved to know why he failed to develop speech and respond to them. They also reported feeling a sense of relief when shown a diagram of the ear revealing the location of the hearing damage. Parents of children and adolescents experiencing emotional and behavioral problems have the same need to know why their children behave as they do. They desperately want to know why these children act differently from others and often refuse to do the things they are expected to do.

Thus, parents and relatives may search their family tree for ancestors with similar problems; attempt to recall the circumstances surrounding accidents and injuries; or debate the impact of a traumatic event such as the death of a family member or friend, or a divorce. Unlike the case involving hearing loss, no simple diagrams exist to explain emotional difficulties. This chapter will examine reasons why children and youth develop emotional and behavioral problems.

How do experts explain emotional problems of children?

A number of scientific theories are used to explain emotional and behavioral problems of children and adolescents. A multitude of not-so-scientific explanations can also be heard, including "bad genes," "bad blood," and "family problems." Just about everyone, including neighbors and in-laws, have an opinion on the matter. Yet, in spite of all this speculation, the exact cause or causes of a child's problems and conflict is rarely known. This does not mean that nothing is known of cause; a good deal is known and more is being learned. However, the exact cause of most emotionally disturbed children's problems remains a mystery. There are several reasons for this lack of clarity: (a) disagreement over the meaning of emotional and behavioral problems; (b) the complexity of human behavior; and (c) the manner in which scientific studies of the causes of emotional and behavioral conditions are conducted.

What does the meaning of an emotional problem have to do with understanding cause?

There is considerable disagreement about what constitutes an emotional or behavioral problem. One parent's "active boy"or "creative individualist" may be another's "behavior-disordered" or "withdrawn" child. This lack of agreement over the meaning of a behavior problem makes it difficult to agree on a cause.

What is meant by the ''complexity of human behavior'' and how does it relate to understanding the cause of a child's problems?

Children respond to their world in a number of ways, some more adaptive than others. Even under the best conditions, different kids will react differently to the same situation. A fifth-grade teacher experienced this when she told her students that one of their classmates had been killed in a weekend automobile accident. Some children wept openly; others gazed off into space; still others rhythmically rocked back and forth in their chairs. The teacher reported that this range of emotion continued for several days. This situation reflects the many ways in which children display their feelings and deal with the events of their world. The complexity of human behavior makes it difficult to accurately understand the relationship between life events and children's behavior.

What's the relation between the manner in which scientific studies are conducted and what is known of cause?

Scientists attempt to look for factors or conditions which may be associated with certain problems. For example, behavior scientists have determined that, on the average, children with learning problems have more school behavioral problems than kids without learning problems. However, this does not mean that learning problems cause behavioral problems. It merely indicates that one condition (learning difficulty) is associated with another condition (behavioral problems). This is a fundamental scientific principle and one that must be carefully considered when evaluating any cause-effect relationship.

An example may help clarify this point. Historians have noted an association between ladies' skirt length and economic depression. However, even the most naive person would be skeptical to assume that such fashion trends cause economic change. Yet, there is an association. As illustrated, an association does not necessarily mean that one thing causes another. Since this type of research (referred to as *correlational*) is a major means by which scientific knowledge about the cause of emotional problems is accumulated, *exact* causes are frequently unknown.

What are the different kinds of causes?

The causes of children's emotional and behavioral problems are best understood by considering two major factors: tendencies to develop certain problems (known as *predisposing factors*) and contributing events (known as *precipitating agents*). *Tendencies* or *predisposing factors* are any conditions which increase a child's risk of developing an emotional problem. Tendencies or predisposing agents may include (but are not limited to) physical illness and disability, shyness, hyperactive behavior, and an emotionally unhealthy home. It is important to note that these conditions are experienced by many children and adolescents, most of whom do not develop emotional problems. Thus, it is incorrect to assume that a child will develop an emotional problem because he has asthma, is shy, or lives in a violent environment. Many mentally healthy persons live useful and healthy lives despite difficult situations. Yet, we must also recognize that these conditions may increase a child's chance of experiencing emotional problems.

Contributing or *precipitating factors* refer to specific incidents which may trigger maladaptive behavior. Included are death, desertion, divorce, or other crisis situations. One 7-year-old who was overly dependent on his parents became at risk for emotional problems when his father deserted the family. While this boy was emotionally able to survive his ordeal, largely as a result of professional counseling, he was susceptible to emotional problems for a period of time. Contributing factors may not be readily apparent (they don't always take such obvious forms as death and divorce). Further, children and adolescents may not show an immediate reaction to a contributing event.

Even when tendencies and contributing factors exist, a child may not develop emotional or behavioral problems. This is one of the confusing aspects of human behavior. Due to individual differences situations produce different reactions. This helps explain why children from the same family act differently, or why seemingly identical children react differently to the same situation.

The causes of emotional and behavioral disturbances are divided into two general categories: biological and environmental. *Biological* refers to physical, medical, and genetic factors. *Environmental* or *psychological* causes, on the other hand, involve those conditions and experiences which make up our day-to-day world.

Family, school, and community conditions are the environmental influences of greatest importance.

How important are biological influences?

All of us are a product of our biology. Our instincts, muscles, nerves, and genetic influences determine, at least to some extent, the manner in which we say, think, and do things. The nervous system, of which the brain is a part, consists of a massive collection of interconnected nerve cells which affect every aspect of life, including our senses and behavior. Thus, some behavior and emotional problems are thought to be the result of biological accidents or influences. Frequently discussed biological causes include genetic influences, neurological impairment (brain damage), body build, nutrition, and physical health.

How important are genetic influences on behavior?

Genetics refers to heredity. Each time a sperm and ovum unite, they merge into a single cell bearing hereditary characteristics from both parents. Anyone doubting the significance of genetic influences need only look as far as the nearest family gathering. Hair color, body shape, facial structure, and other physical characteristics will link children to their parents and parents to their ancestors. Nonphysical characteristics may also be influenced by genetic factors, including intelligence and temperament.

Genetic influences have long been used to explain emotional and behavioral problems. Comments such as "He gets so angry and irrational, just like his father did when he was that age."; and "It's no wonder Joan is such a problem in school; she inherited the same bad genes as her older brothers." While such statements may be inviting, they are usually inaccurate. When we assume that children and adolescents demonstrate the same behavioral patterns, either positive or negative, as other family members, we frequently overlook the powerful influence of environment and numerous other conditions which affect behavior. For example, if a child of shy parents demonstrates a lack of interest in people, it is difficult to know if this behavior pattern is a result of modeling, heredity, or other conditions. Behavior may be influenced by genetic factors. However, there is little reason to assume that heredity is the primary cause of behavior. In many instances, environmental factors appear to be the principal influence.

There are indications that genetic influences are closely associated with certain types of mental illness. In particular, schizophrenia (a severe form of mental illness characterized by extreme withdrawal, reduced functioning capacity, hallucinations, and delusions) has been found to be more common among blood relatives. Although schizophrenia occurs in less than 1% of the general population, the risk of the condition increases proportionately with the degree of blood relationship one has with a diagnosed schizophrenic. For example, the rate of schizophrenia among children who have one schizophrenic parent is about 15% while having two schizophrenic parents increases the probability to about 40%. Although home environment must be considered in interpreting these statistics, a sufficient number of studies have controlled home influences (such as cases where identical twins have been reared in separate homes) to warrant the suggestion that genetics is associated with this form of mental illness.

A male genetic variation consisting of an extra Y chromosome has been associated with overly aggressive characteristics. However, because the scientific study of genetic influences is only in its infancy, it is difficult to evaluate the impact of genetics on behavior. Thus, in spite of indications of genetic influence, especially in severe emotional disturbance, more evidence must be collected before final conclusions can be drawn. Further, even when hereditary influences are associated with emotional problems they are usually only a partial explanation of cause.

What about brain damage as a cause of emotional disturbance?

The term *neurological impairment*, or *brain damage*, is both threatening and confusing. One need only think about the term for a moment before frightening images appear. Neurological injuries range from severe destruction of tissue, resulting in death or serious disability, to tiny injuries producing little or no behavior change.

It has long been assumed that damage to the brain and its wrappings is associated with childhood emotional and behavioral problems. However, neither the meaning of *neurological impairment* nor its influence as a cause of emotional problems has been agreed upon. Brain damage suggests dysfunction due to injury. The damage may be to brain cells (neurons), glia (non-brain cell material), or blood vessels. If severe, such damage may lead to loss or deterioration of certain fuctions (e.g., vision, coordination). Damage may occur as a result of anoxia (lack of oxygen), physical injury, high fever, infection, or toxins such as poison or drugs.

Neurological impairment may be permanent or reversible. Neurological impairment is considered to be relatively common; in most cases, however, it is inconsequential. Nearly every parent and teacher have discovered that children fall and bang into things, usually with no discernible long-term effect. In one often-quoted medical study of newborn children, examination of spinal fluid one week after birth revealed evidence of blood in half the infants. Blood in this context indicated that some degree of trauma had occurred to the brain or its wrappings in the birth process. However, since most of the infants in the study grew to become healthy children, it is relatively safe to assume that this problem was either minimal or reversible. This conclusion is not an attempt to minimize the importance of neurological impairment. Although brain damage can result in serious and permanent disability, most instances of alleged neurological impairment do not entail severe or permanent consequences. Further, there is limited evidence to suggest that such problems are associated with behavioral and emotional difficulties.

Hard and *soft* signs are commonly used to describe neurological conditions. A *hard* sign refers to specific neurological damage responsible for a particular problem or deficit. For example, a child with an identifiable injury (referred to as a *lesion*) may experience uncontrolled, jerky, and irregular motor movements. *Soft* damage, on the other hand, refers to an alleged minimal and unidentifiable injury. While the actual damage cannot be identified, it is assumed to exist because of certain behaviors thought to develop in relation to the extent and location of the injury, a child's personality, and environmental influences. The most common terms associated with soft damage are *minimal brain dysfunction* and *attention deficit disorder*. These terms are used to describe children who demonstrate hyperactivity, learning problems, distractibility, perceptual difficulties, and clumsiness.

An example of a child thought to demonstrate minimal brain dysfunction was a 10-year-old boy named Todd. Although of average intelligence, Todd experienced difficulty in school. His teachers reported that he was easily distracted, fidgety, unpredictable, difficult to discipline, unpopular with his peers, and frequently failed to finish assignments. His parents noted the same sorts of problems at home. Consequently, Todd was referred for an evaluation, the results of which indicated that he might be minimally brain damaged. However, the physician who conducted the evaluation expressed to Todd's parents and teacher that the diagnosis was questionable and speculative. Such a conclusion has been echoed by many professionals.

While the influence of brain damage must not be overlooked, it is important to carefully consider its significance. First, the relationship between brain damage and emotional disturbance has not been clearly established. Brain damage can and does produce abnormal behavior. However, it cannot automatically be concluded that emotional and behavioral problems result from neurological difficulties. This conclusion is based on the finding that the vast majority of behaviorally and emotionally disturbed children and adolescents do not show convincing signs of neurological impairment. Although brain damage may be a factor in the development of some emotional problems, it does not appear to be a major cause.

Is body build really associated with emotional and behavioral problems?

Body build as an explanation for emotional problems, often referred to as *constitutional*, is based on the notion that individuals with different physiques (body build) display different temperaments and are more or less vulnerable to certain types of problems. Tradition has typed the plump person as happy-go-lucky and lazy, in contrast to the thin individual who is generally portrayed as sly and suspicious. These stereotypes are clearly shown by Shakespeare in the play *Julius Caesar:*

Let me have men about me that are fat,
Sleek-headed men, and such as sleep o'nights:
Yond Cassius has a lean and hungry look,
He thinks too much: such men are dangerous.

In spite of literature and folklore, there is limited evidence to suggest that a person's build is a cause of emotional problems. Nonetheless, body build may be associated with particular types of problems. One example is the tendency of juvenile delinquents to have muscular builds. This may mean that physical strength and a muscular physique are needed to be a successful delinquent. That is, it is probably more difficult for a thin and weak or a heavy and slow adolescent to be accepted by a gang of delinquent youths and to be involved in aggressive acts.

Are there other biological causes of emotional disturbance?

A number of biological causes of emotional disturbance have been suggested. Some of these are thought to have some validity, but most are nothing more than myths (e.g., inhaling tobacco fumes and bathing in cold water cause emotional problems). From this vast number of theories, two will be discussed: nutritional factors and physical health.

There is no doubt that malnutrition is associated with learning problems, and, in some instances, emotional problems. Kids who are malnourished possess neither the strength nor the motivation to do well in school or to display acceptable behaviors. In extreme cases malnutrition may cause brain damage and mental retardation.

In addition, certain foods, particularly refined sugar, food additives, and food dye, are thought by some to cause hyperactivity and other behavioral problems. While definite conclusions have not been drawn in this area, certain children may indeed respond poorly to specific foods.

Children and adolescents with severe, long-term health problems and physical handicaps may suffer from emotional problems including depression, anger, and suicidal tendencies. As with other possible causes, this does not mean that all such children will experience these problems, or that such conditions *cause* emotional difficulties. However, health problems and physical handicaps do cause additional stress, and, in some instances, are thought to result in emotional conflicts.

What kinds of conclusions can be drawn about biological causes of emotional disturbance?

There is no question that biological conditions may contribute to behavioral and emotional problems. In particular, genetic accidents, brain damage, malnutrition, and physical illness and impairment may increase children's susceptibility to certain types of difficulties. However, most behaviorally disordered and emotionally disturbed children and adolescents do not have problems *exclusively* because of biological factors. At best, these contribute to emotional problems.

What is meant by "environmental" cause?

Environment is everything external to a child. Thus, environmental cause relates to the notion that a child's world, including home experiences, parent and family relationships, community, and school experiences influence mental health. This view should come as no surprise since it is apparent that the values, attitudes, experiences, and expectations to which children are exposed affect their behavior. Thus, children who are exposed to unhealthy conditions are thought to be more susceptible to emotional problems.

How important are parental and family influences on a child's mental health?

The family, typically consisting of mother, father, and children, has long been considered a primary determinant of a child's personality development and mental health. Parents have the potential to be with their school-age children about two-thirds of every day during the school year and all day weekends and vacations. It is no wonder, then, that parents and other family members are important to children's development by helping them develop their views of the world and their self-concepts. Therefore, the question of whether less-than-favorable experiences contribute to emotional and behavioral problems is logical.

It is important to recognize (and accept) that children's problems are not always caused by parents and families. This is not to suggest that parents and families do not have a significant influence on children nor that some cases of emotional disturbance and behavior problems can be attributed to parents. Yet, in numerous cases children and youth develop problems of which parents are not the cause. Yet, society is quick to blame parents for their offspring's problems. Even professionals, on occasion, have been guilty of this offense. For example, several years ago it was popular to assume that parents' interactions with and attitudes toward their children were the cause of autism (a severe developmental disability characterized by language delays, retardation, and social withdrawal). This allegation has absolutely no truth. The simple fact is that there is overwhelming evidence to suggest that children's problems are not always attributable to parents.

What sorts of family experiences may affect children and adolescents?

Several conditions or experiences may influence the behavior and emotional status of children. In particular, conditions which increase parent, family, or children's stress is important, including economic problems, relocation to new cities, parent career changes, role changes (e.g., a mother who takes a full-time job out of the home), and similar situations. Readers should recognize that change is not necessarily negative, however. Just because a mother chooses to take a job or a career opportunity that necessitates a move, it does not mean that children will suffer. Yet, such changes may increase stress, at least temporarily, and some children may react negatively.

An example involves a family, consisting of a mother, father, and three elementary-age children, who experienced severe economic problems and subsequent family changes. The family owned and operated a small farm in the midwest. As many farmers in this decade, the family fell behind in their bank payments and faced what appeared to be loss of their farm. The father experienced extreme depression over his plight and subsequently was forced to take a job he disliked and considered demeaning. His wife, who had never worked outside the home, took a job as an aide in a nursing home, a position she also disliked. The children, for the first time in their lives, were without adult supervision for periods of time in the afternoon. Further, they were regularly exposed to their parents' feelings, anxieties, and stresses. Subsequently, one of the children, an 8-year-old boy, developed academic and behavioral problems at school. He also demonstrated fear of abandonment and severe anxiety at home. The youngster's problems were dealt with in part through counseling provided by the school; however, significant improvement did not occur until his parents' financial situation improved.

The above example illustrates the potential impact of family experiences on children. Not every child or adolescent will be effected; however, awareness of and sensitivity to the potential of such conditions is important.

What kind of effect does divorce have on children?

Not surprisingly, two-parent homes characterized by harmony and good will tend to have a positive influence on children. Such homes, however, do not protect children and adolescents from emotional and behavioral problems. Even the best homes may have problem children. In a similar fashion, many children from single-parent families adjust well to their circumstances. Thus, while experts agree that separation and divorce are seldom good experiences, these events do not always lead to problems.

The impact of divorce on children and adolescents has been widely debated. While there continues to be more questions than answers some patterns may be discerned. First, children seem to respond to the breakup of their families not only in accordance with their unique personalities but also their age and sex. That is, young children respond differently from older children and boys often differently from girls. Further, children usually experience distress over a divorce or separation regardless of the amount of discord and anxiety that existed prior to the separation. That is, contrary to the popular notion that children are relieved following the departure of one parent, the opposite often is true. In fact, relief is only common when an abusive parent leaves the home. Further, the relationship that existed between the children and the parent who is leaving is frequently unrelated to the degree to which children are upset over the breakup of their family. In many cases, children's sadness over a separation or divorce is associated with their grief and anxiety over the breakup of their family rather than how close they were to the departing parent.

What kinds of responses do children at various ages show to divorce?

Children of all ages may show a number of emotional reactions to their parents' separation and divorce, including sadness, anger, depression, shame, guilt, fear, and rejection. It is also common for children to try and reunite their parents, thus restoring the family.

Babies and toddlers will not understand the divorce and separation process. Yet, because they are so dependent on their parents, and so responsive to their moods and anxieties, they will probably be affected. The mother of a 2-year-old became concerned over her son's loss of appetite and withdrawn behavior. Whereas he was generally playful and friendly, the boy's behavior changed dramatically after his parents' separation. Because the father's travel schedule had given the child only limited contact with his father during the year before the separation, the mother did not think her son was responding to his father's absence. Counseling revealed that the mother was unprepared for her husband's desire to leave the family and that she was experiencing a great deal of anxiety and depression as a result. It also became clear that the child was responding to his mother's depression and anxiety rather than his father's absence.

Preschoolers often blame themselves for their parents' problems and may take personal responsibility for separation and divorce. Some preschoolers will attempt to behave like angels so that the parent who left might feel committed to return. Other young children show immature behavior, including anger and sadness. The anger of boys is more commonly expressed as acting-out behavior, whereas girls are apt to turn their anger inward, leading to withdrawal and pouting. A 5-year-old girl who was usually outgoing and friendly became a concern when she began to withdraw from her friends to be by herself. This change occurred shortly after her parents' divorce and continued for several months.

For 6- to 8-year-olds, whose self-concept and security are based on the strength of their family, divorce is likely to lead to feelings of sadness, fear, helplessness, and deprivation. These children may also work hard to restore their family. A recently divorced mother noted that after returning from weekend visits with his father, her son would write to him pleading for his return. In his letters the boy wrote of the love he and his mother had for him and how he longed for the family to be back together. The mother, who had no interest in reuniting with her former husband, observed that the child had not been close to his father before the divorce but seemed preoccupied with getting the family together after the separation.

Pre-adolescents are usually able to understand that a divorce is based on their parents' problems. Nonetheless, these children react to a divorce, most commonly with displays of anger—sometimes so strong as to cloud underlying feelings of sadness and helplessness. Such anger is often related to feelings that the rules of fair play and loyalty, which the youngsters were taught by their parents, are not being followed. It is also not unusual for these children to align with one parent against the other or to feel caught in a loyalty conflict between two parents.

It may also be difficult for pre-adolescents to deal with their parents' dating. Thus, their struggle to understand and develop their own sexual identity may be complicated by their parents' sexual role change. One mother who had been divorced for 18 months said she was horrified at her 12-year-old daughter's behavior. The girl blamed her mother for numerous things, including her inability to do well in school and attract friends. She was also opposed to her mother dating, and reportedly tried to drive men away.

For teenagers, such typical problems as rebellion, emotional changes, and struggles for independence may be heightened by divorce or separation. Some younger teens may experience guilt over their parents' problems, although most seem to be able to separate themselves from their parents' conflict. Nonetheless, the strong emotions of adolescence may intensify feelings of shame, anger, betrayal, and embarrassment that typically follow a divorce.

It should again be noted that children of all ages will be affected by parental separation and divorce. However, such an event does not automatically lead to emotional and behavioral problems. The notion that divorce and separation *directly cause* emotional and behavioral problems in children and adolescents is unfounded.

Are children affected by the problems of their parents following a divorce?

Children and adolescents can be expected to respond, to varying degrees, to the emotional and personal problems of the adults in their lives during the difficult period of a separation and divorce. Adults going through these stages often feel a sense of failure, anger, stress, anxiety, and loss of self-esteem. Thus, at times when children may most require the support of their parents, these individuals may be so involved in their own problems that they are of limited help. Further, children may be drawn into disputes between feuding parents.

Three major groups of problems experienced by adults during separation and divorce may affect children and adolescents: financial problems; family management concerns; and personal problems.

A major concern of many single parents, especially mothers, is economic survival. According to a number of surveys, the income of families headed by single mothers is less than half that of father-headed homes. Further, over half the children in single-parent homes headed by mothers live below the poverty level. Not only do some mothers find it necessary to seek employment for the first time, often without the benefit of marketable skills, but child support payments from fathers are often irregular or nonexistent. Such economic problems can be expected to reduce the standard of living of many homes, a change for which children may hold their custodial parent (the parent with legal child custody) personally responsible.

One recently divorced woman said she had been unprepared for the financial problems she was to face after her divorce. Even when she was able to find full-time employment, her income was only a fraction of what she and her children had been accustomed to live on. In spite of her explanations, her children held her responsible for their life-style change.

Custodial parents may also experience management problems related to increased responsibility and other changes which typically accompany a divorce. For example, mothers may find that in addition to working full time they are still responsible for all the chores (and maybe more) they had while they were married. Parents may also find their children harder to discipline following a divorce. Some children are inclined to test their parents after a divorce to see if family rules still exist and if they will be enforced. Some custodial parents are described by their children as being more restrictive, less affectionate, and more inconsistent in their discipline than noncustodial parents (particularly fathers), who tend to be permissive and indulgent.

The three children of one recently divorced woman complained that their mother treated them unfairly and accused her of being stricter than before her divorce. After several discussions with her children, the mother confessed that she did not want to fail with her children in the same way she had failed in her marriage. Consequently, she had chosen rigid rule enforcement as a means of accomplishing this goal. After these discussions, she became more flexible in dealing with her children, and her kids, in turn, became more sensitive to their mother's needs.

It is also not uncommon for divorced parents to experience isolation and discrimination at a time when they are most in need of support. Not surprisingly, the feelings of anger, depression, and lowered self-esteem which accompany these experiences may affect their children's attitude and behavior.

What conclusions can be drawn about the relationship between divorce and children's emotional problems?

The question of whether divorce causes emotional and behavioral problems in children is not easily answered. On the one hand, experts agree that divorce does have a significant effect, seldom of a positive nature. Is it safe, therefore, to conclude that divorce causes emotional disturbance? The answer is *No!* Although separation and divorce may be potential contributors to emotional problems, these events have not been shown to *cause* emotional disturbance. Even though most children and adolescents whose parents divorce do not become emotionally disturbed, they will probably experience some distress.

Are parents with problems of their own and those who expose their kids to unhealthy psychological conditions more apt to have emotionally disturbed children?

Parents' personal problems, especially in combination with an unhealthy home environment, may contribute to children's emotional disturbance. Thus, unstable and inconsistent parents more commonly have children with emotional and behavioral problems. Not all children and adolescents develop emotional and behavioral problems because of these conditions. However, certain parental and family patterns and events—both positive and negative—can make children more susceptible to emotional problems. For example, hostile and aggressive children are more common in hostile and aggressive families. This does not necessarily mean that hostile family interactions cause hostility in children. On the contrary, it is possible, for example, for children with emotional and behavioral problems to cause families to behave in a hostile and aggressive manner.

The way in which parents discipline their children has long been thought to relate to children's mental health. As one might guess, parents who are warm and loving and who consistently and fairly discipline their kids seem to get the best results. Hostile and inconsistent methods of discipline, in contrast, are thought to be the least effective, and the most apt to produce problems in children. Most kids are able to adapt as long as rules and rule enforcement are consistent and fair. Thus, many experts believe that children are most secure knowing that rules exist and that the adults in their lives are concerned enough to place limits on their behavior. The children in one family confided to their parents that they liked knowing family rules. They said they were enticed by the freedom enjoyed by the children in one neighborhood family, but felt secure knowing their parents cared enough to establish realistic rules.

There is no doubt that parents and families do play a part in children's behavior and mental health. For example, a child or adolescent's chances of becoming delinquent are increased by living in a disorganized home (*disorganized* refers to lax and inconsistent rule setting and enforcement) and families where parents have been in prison. In a similar fashion, children who have been physically and sexually abused can be expected to evidence more psychological problems than other children. Although we cannot automatically conclude that such homes will always produce children with problems, neither can we dismiss their potential negative influence.

Do children and youth with emotional and behavioral problems respond in the same way in different settings?

The answer to this question is no. There are numerous examples of children and adolescents who are behaviorally disordered at school but who demonstrate acceptable behavior at home and in the community. Similarly, some children whose parents find extremely difficult to control at home seem to avoid problems at school. Thus, although many children with behavioral and emotional problems can be expected to encounter difficulty in a variety of settings, there are exceptions.

There are several possible explanations for such differences. One is related to expectation. That is, children are expected to do different things at school and at home. For example, a child may be motivated and good at doing chores at home but poor at completing academic assignments at school. For such a youngster, school-related conflict will be more common than home conflict.

Another explanation relates to structure. Some children are able to do well at school but not at home because of clearly stated school rules and consequences. One 11-year-old, for example, related that he did "pretty good in school" because his teacher clearly stated and enforced behavioral limits and consequences, conditions which did not exist when he went home.

A final explanation of variations in responses is related to definition. That is, school personnel and parents may not agree on what constitutes a problem. For example, regular use of profanity may be considered a problem at school while at home such language may be accepted.

What conclusions can be drawn about the relationship between emotional disturbance and parent/family conditions?

In spite of strong indications that certain parent and family conditions may *contribute*, either positively or negatively, to children's
personality and social development, there is no clearcut evidence
that such events are the *cause* of emotional and behavioral problems. It must be remembered that each child's behavior is the
result of a complex interaction of personality, temperament, and
the various experiences which make up the environment. Given
these differences, it is easy to understand why each child
responds in a unique way.

Are there things schools and communities do to reduce or cause emotional problems?

When children or adolescents are not with their family, they are
apt to be in school or elsewhere in the community. Thus, schools
and communities have the potential to either further or hinder
children's emotional development.

While other aspects of a child's world may be chaotic and
unhealthy, school is usually considered a positive influence. Yet,
even schools are sometimes potential contributors to children's
problems.

One way in which schools may contribute to children's problems is by failing to accommodate individual needs and personalities. Because they serve large groups of children, schools
tend to aim learning experiences toward the average student.
As a result, each fourth grader usually uses the same books,
receives the same instruction and is exposed to the same experiences. In essence, the student is treated like every other student
in that grade. Obviously, students in the same grade are not the
same. They vary in intelligence, maturity, skills, experiences, and
ability. Thus, when children are treated the same with only
limited accommodation for differences, those with even minor
problems may be considered misfits. For example, even though

all third-grade boys and girls are expected to read at the third-grade level, individual differences exist. Children who read below the designated level will probably be required to use the same text as pupils reading at or above grade level, leading to a lower self-image for underachieving students who are unable to reach some set standard. The resulting frustration and failure may help explain why some of these children misbehave or withdraw. Consequently, by failing to treat children as individuals, schools may promote problems. Teachers may rightfully contend that large class sizes and other restrictions make it unrealistic to carry out individual planning. Yet, such conditions may contribute to students' emotional and behavioral problems.

Schools may also contribute to emotional and behavioral problems of children and youth by failing to provide the best teachers. As frequently noted in the press, the quality of American education has declined. Currently, the most important job in our society—educating young people—is often carried out by individuals who are not the most qualified. This is not an indictment of all teachers. There are many excellent educators whose dedication and hard work enable them to create the conditions required for educational growth and development. Yet, only the most uninformed would fail to recognize that education has suffered over the past decades and that the highest quality teachers are not always available. Most children and adolescents adjust to mediocre teachers, but those students who are most vulnerable to problems may not. By failing to encourage the most capable individuals to enter and stay in the teaching profession, our educational system may place vulnerable students in jeopardy.

Schools may further contribute to students' problems by inconsistent rules and policies. Children and adolescents who are most susceptible to emotional and behavioral problems are best served by clearly stated rules and conditions. Although children and adolescents are reluctant to agree, they generally benefit from consistent enforcement of rules and absence of the unpredictability that often characterizes parts of their world, such as home life. By failing to provide the necessary structure and consistency schools may contribute to emotional and behavioral problems.

Finally, school personnel may contribute to children's problems by not striving to communicate and cooperate with parents. In spite of advances in this area, teacher-parent relationships are often less than adequate. Although not totally a school problem, this issue can affect children. In instances of mistrust and absence of parent-teacher communication, children and adolescents prone to problems become more vulnerable.

What is the relationship between emotional and behavioral problems and communities?

Towns and cities which provide adequate recreational facilities and other opportunities for young people to spend time together are most apt to foster good behavioral and emotional development. Further, communities which offer adequate mental health services and counseling are best able to deal with those problems which arise in the course of everyday living. Without suitable social agencies, psychological services, and counseling programs, even minor problems may become serious.

Summary

Identification of exact causes of emotional and behavioral problems is complex. A variety of possible reasons exist. While each explanation may have some validity, no single reason can be pinpointed as *the* cause. By looking at our own family members and friends we recognize that everyone has unique ways of adjusting to the world. Our ways of adjusting are based on both biological and environmental mechanisms. Because of each person's individuality and a multitude of biological and environmental influences, it is no wonder that the causes of emotional and behavioral problems are so difficult to identify.

How Do We Identify Children and Youth with Emotional and Behavioral Problems?

3

Psychologists, psychiatrists, and educators usually determine which children and adolescents are emotionally disturbed. Using methods which are often poorly understood by the public, these professionals attempt to identify treatment and educational plans for children and youth who require special educational and mental health programs and services. Mental health professionals and educators experience little difficulty determining that persons who demonstrate bizarre, highly irrational, and other extremely deviant behavior over an extended period of time are disturbed. However, since the problems of most children and youth with emotional and behavioral problems are more subtle the identification process tends to be complex with this group of individuals. This chapter will focus on methods used to identify and diagnose children and adolescents with emotional and behavioral problems.

What are the purposes of an evaluation?

Evaluations are rarely carried out for the sole purpose of finding out whether or not a child is disturbed. Rather, assessment is designed to provide information about each child's psychological and educational strengths and weaknesses; unique ways of dealing with the world; and possible problem-solving and treatment options. At the same time, one of the expected outcomes of such an evaluation is that a professional judgment will be made regarding a child's or adolescent's emotional and behavioral health. Thus, in addition to providing an educational and psychological understanding of a child and recommending appropriate treatment methods, mental health and educational professionals must determine if a youngster is evidencing a true emotional or behavioral problem.

What is meant by a "true" emotional problem?

Not every child or adolescent who violates school, home, or community rules or who displays behavior that is of concern to an adult has an emotional problem. Such problems may be the result of short-term troubles, normal individual differences, or a host of other factors. For example, a child whose parents worry because he does not spend enough time playing with other children could be (a) passing through a phase; (b) demonstrating a unique, yet normal, personality trait; or (c) showing any one of a number of normal behavior patterns. As a result of the numerous explanations for children's behavior and the subtlety of most emotional problems, mental health and school personnel are often called upon to make fine emotional-fitness discriminations. To further complicate the process, such discriminations are frequently based on imprecise measurement methods.

Don't psychological tests give precise information about children's mental health?

Even today the diagnostic methods available to psychologists and psychiatrists are not only poorly understood, many believe they are as much an art as a science. Such conditions may explain why it is not unusual for persons, including professionals, to disagree on the exact nature and significance of children's problems.

If tests and procedures aren't exact, why should an assessment be conducted?

As indicated, evaluation of a child's personality and emotional status is not easy and seldom leads to a clearcut conclusion about the presence of an emotional problem. Further, as publicized in the media, the accuracy of such diagnostic procedures has been subjected to much criticism. In the words of some of the world's most respected mental health professionals, the evaluation process is an imperfect science. Yet, in spite of their limitations, evaluations are important as a necessary step toward appropriate services.

There are a number of reasons for conducting evaluations with children, one of which is to assure that children and adolescents receive appropriate treatment and intervention. That is, assessment is not only undertaken to determine the nature and degree of a child's problems, but to identify suitable treatment and problem-solving options. Since these plans are individualized on the basis of each child's strengths and weaknesses, they must be developed through an evaluation. Simply stated, an appropriate educational or treatment plan requires accurate and complete assessment information.

Are there other reasons for conducting evaluations?

Yes, one of them is to ensure that the limited mental health and educational resources available to children and adolescents are provided to those most needing them. This is not meant to imply that mental health and school personnel should not do preventive work. Rather, programs and resources must be reserved for those children and youth most able to benefit from them.

Another reason for conducting evaluations relates to the existence of normal individual differences. Simply because a child responds "differently" or fails to do something in exactly the same way as another person does not mean that he or she is emotionally disturbed. One of the benefits of assessment is that it gives an objective report of whether or not a particular difference is psychologically significant. In his 1961 book, *Welcome to the Monkeyhouse*, Kurt Vonnegut, Jr., skillfully pointed out the reality of human differences and the absurdity of expecting everyone to look and act the same. Vonnegut observed:

> The year was 2081, and everybody was finally equal. They weren't only equal before God and the law. They were equal every which way. Nobody was smarter than anybody else. Nobody was better looking than anybody else. All this equality was due to the 211th, 212th and 213th Amendments to the Constitution, and to the unceasing vigilance of agents of the United States Handicapped General.[1]

In this excerpt, Vonnegut reminds us that differences in human characteristics and behavior are to be expected. Although certain deviations may be so significant as to require professional attention, their presence must be identified by qualified persons.

What is meant by "screening"?

The process of selecting children and adolescents for a thorough evaluation is known as *screening*. Complete evaluations of these children and youth should reveal the nature of the assumed difficulties and help identify the most suitable treatment. Unlike routine medical and dental checkups, mental health evaluations are conducted only with children and adolescents whose behavior attracts attention—usually from parents and teachers—due to excesses or deficits. *Excesses*, meaning too much of a given behavior, usually involve aggressiveness, impulsiveness, antisocial behavior, acting-out, disruptiveness, and similar acts. In contrast, behavioral *deficits*, or too little of a desired behavior, include social withdrawal, shyness, and timidity.

---

[1]Vonnegut, K. (1961). *Welcome to the monkeyhouse (p.7)*. New York: Dell.

How important is accurate screening?

Screening which fails to accurately identify children for further study may interfere with delivery of needed services. That is, if screening techniques do not identify children and adolescents who require additional educational and psychological evaluation, such youngsters will probably be denied services. On the other hand, procedures which incorrectly select children and adolescents for further evaluation can cause overloads for those professionals responsible for conducting evaluations and emotional stress for the children and their families.

Who carries out the screening?

Screening is primarily carried out by parents and teachers. Although pediatricians, principals, clergy, family friends, and others may aid in seeking services, teachers and parents carry out the majority of this work.

How good are teachers and parents at screening children and adolescents for emotional problems?

Studies have shown that teachers are very effective at identifying children and adolescents with problems significant enough to warrant assessment. These individuals may occasionally use formal educational procedures to aid in the identification; however, more commonly they rely on their own experience, observation skills, and professional intuition.

Parents can also be effective at determining if their children require professional attention. Not only do parents have more contact, relevant history, and intimate knowledge about their offspring than anybody else, they are usually more committed to securing the best possible services and programs.

Who are the persons who conduct evaluations?

Professionals representing a variety of disciplines (specific professions) are involved in an evaluation. These persons may be associated with schools or mental health agencies. The following is a listing of some of these professionals along with a description of their role in the assessment process.

Psychologists: School and clinical psychologists collect and interpret information about intellectual ability, personality characteristics, academic achievement level, and perceptual and neurological strengths and weaknesses. Psychologists use tests, parent and child interviews, and direct observations.

Psychiatrists: Psychiatrists are concerned with many of the same areas as psychologists. However, psychiatrists rely more on interviews and direct observations of behavior than tests. Because they hold medical degrees (MD or DO) they may prescribe medications for children, if necessary.

Educators: Educators test academic strengths and weaknesses and conditions under which learning is best achieved. They use tests as well as observation and interview techniques.

Social workers: Both school and psychiatric social workers perform a variety of functions. However, their primary job is to serve as a link between evaluation personnel and families, schools, and community agencies. Social workers not only attempt to provide other diagnostic personnel with a complete history of a given child, they also try to obtain relevant information from such sources as legal authorities, welfare workers, and clergy.

Speech pathologists: These professionals are involved in evaluations only under certain circumstances. For example, in instances where there are no apparent speech or language problems they may serve a minor role. Speech pathologists use a variety of tests and procedures to determine the manner in which children receive and process messages, and how children and adolescents express themselves.

Audiologists: These professionals participate in evaluations when a child's ability to hear is questioned. Where indicated, they use a number of methods and testing procedures to assess children's ability to hear.

Physical therapists: These professionals use tests as well as their own observational skills to assess physical ability and muscle control. They are most likely to participate in evaluations involving neurological or perceptual problems.

Occupational therapists: Although these staff members appear to be dealing with the same areas as physical therapists, they are more concerned with assessing self-help, daily-living and similar skills. They use both observational and testing methods.

Medical personnel: When necessary, medical professionals including nurses, pediatricians, neurologists, family practitioners, and optometrists are involved in evaluations. These individuals' specialty skills add to a more thorough understanding of children and youth.

What does an evaluation involve?

A child's problems, abilities, and behaviors can only be analyzed through a complete and comprehensive evaluation. *Complete* here means that a variety of individuals representing several professional disciplines (e.g., psychologists, educators, and audiologists) are involved; *comprehensive* refers to the use of an array of procedures and techniques to gain a thorough understanding of a child. Evaluations may be carried out by either school or community personnel. Even though school personnel tend to put more emphasis on educational matters than mental health professionals, both groups provide effective evaluations. Since both school and community professionals provide diagnostic and assessment services it is important for these groups to work together. Such cooperation usually results in more effective understanding and treatment of emotionally and behaviorally troubled children and youth. Further, it is becoming increasingly necessary for professionals from these groups to work together during evaluations.

What techniques are used to evaluate children and adolescents and what information do they yield?

A variety of techniques and procedures may be used to assess behavior-problem children and adolescents. Such procedures give information in the following areas: *intellectual/cognitive; environmental/ecological; physical/medical; emotional*; and *educational*. Although a number of other areas are suitable for assessment, these are considered the most significant and relevant.

What is intellectual/cognitive ability?

There are subtle and technical differences between intellectual and cognitive abilities. However, for all practical purposes the terms are used interchangeably to refer to the mental abilities by which children and adolescents gain knowledge and interact with their world.

How is intellectual ability measured?

A variety of tests are available for assessing intelligence and cognitive ability. These tests can be divided into two general categories: group and individual scales. For the most part, group tests are pencil-and-paper scales, administered by written or oral directions of a trained examiner to a group of children or adolescents. Typically, these measures are used for large-group assessment, as might be required for induction into the military or admission to a college or university. Although group tests may be used during screening they are rarely suited for evaluation purposes.

Individualized tests, on the other hand, are designed for use with one person at a time. These tests, which must also be administered by a professionally trained examiner, are designed to evaluate cognitive and intellectual abilities and to allow comparison between individual results and those of a group of other persons of similar age and characteristics. The comparison group is referred to as a *standardization sample* or *standardization group*. Through the use of such standardization groups, a child can be compared on intelligence and related abilities to other children of the same age.

How are standardization groups used to judge children's ability?

When placed on a graph, intelligence test scores produce a bell-shaped curve (Figure 3.1). Imagine, for example, that all students in a school system were given an intelligence test. If their scores were placed on a graph with a baseline ranging from the highest to the lowest IQ scores and another line representing the number of students with a particular score, a large hump would appear in the middle of the curve and taper off at the ends. As shown, this bell-shaped curve simply means that the largest number of intelligence test scores would fall in the middle (average range) of the curve whereas high and low scores would be represented at the ends. Over half the students would be expected to demonstrate average intellectual ability (IQs between 90 and 110) whereas only about 2% of those tested would score in the superior range (130 and above) or in the intellectually deficient range (IQs of 70 and below).

Why is it important to consider intellectual ability?

Since children and adolescents with behavioral and emotional problems often have difficulty acquiring information and skills,

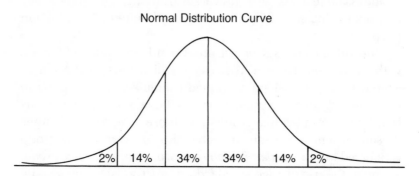

Figure 3.1. *Percent of cases by portion of normal distribution.*

evaluation of their intellectual abilities is important. Further, intellectual ability is considered one of the best predictors of a child's overall prognosis (a prediction of future outcome). While there are exceptions, most emotionally and behaviorally disordered children and adolescents will score lower than their nonhandicapped peers, although both groups' scores fall within the near-average range (IQs of 85-115).

What tests are used to evaluate IQ?

The most widely used individualized intelligence tests are the Wechsler series. *The Wechsler Preschool and Primary Scale of Intelligence* (WPPSI) is designed for children between the ages of 4–6; the *Revised Wechsler Intelligence Scale for Children* (WISC-R) is aimed at children and adolescents 6–17; and the *Revised Wechsler Adult Intelligence Scale* (WAIS) at youth 17 and older. Each of these tests yields three separate IQ scores: a verbal IQ, a performance IQ, and a full-scale score (an IQ score based on a combined verbal and performance IQ). As suggested in the name, the verbal scales focus on such areas as vocabulary, fund of general information, and ability to understand social situations. In contrast, the performance areas do not require verbal answers, but target such skills as forming designs with blocks and putting together puzzle pieces.

Professionals conducting intellectual evaluations are interested in far more than a child's mere intelligence. Type and quality of answers as well as behavioral observations, for example, are just as significant for the overall assessment. Thus, one psychologist noted that an adolescent became extremely upset whenever time demands were introduced. When asked about his behavior at a later time the youth answered, "I don't like people telling me what to do and how much time I have to do it."

What is environmental/ecological assessment?

This assessment area covers environmental factors which influence behavior. That is, attention has shifted from influences on behavior which are a part of the child (e.g., personality and genetic history) to factors which are outside the child, such as parents, family, and other environmental conditions. An understanding of these influences provides a thorough understanding of children and their problems.

How is environmental/ecological information obtained?

The most frequently used means of obtaining environmental and ecological information is a parental (or legal custodian) interview. Because parents have more intimate contact with and possess relevant history about their child they are the logical source of such information. Further, parents tend to be more motivated and have more legal rights to be involved in the evaluation than anybody else. Evaluation personnel may also study community characteristics and conditions and other factors which may influence a child's behavior or attitude (e.g., presence of neighborhood youth gangs, recreational and leisure resources).

What's involved in a parent interview?

Although each parent interview will have its own emphasis and objectives, certain elements are universal. First, interviewers can be expected to begin by asking parents to share information about their child's alleged problem and the degree to which it is a concern. Parental impressions will be sought before parents are offered examples of other people's impressions of the alleged problem. This strategy is used to prevent parental responses from being tainted by others' impressions. In instances where parents make referrals this approach rarely creates problems. That is, when parents seek assistance because of an alleged emotional or behavioral problem they usually wish to share their perceptions. However, the situation may be different when parents are told that their child may have a problem and that an evaluation is consequently needed. Under such conditions parents may be more interested in learning why someone considers their child to have a problem than in offering information about a condition of which they may not be aware. In such situations, for example, when school personnel make the contact, parents should be provided with the background of the alleged problem.

Parents should also expect being asked about their child's developmental history during an interview. Questions will cover significant events, beginning with the mother's pregnancy and continuing to the present. In particular, emotional stress or unusual circumstances during pregnancy; delivery problems; illnesses, accidents and complications; and the age at which developmental milestones (e.g., walking, toilet training, and speech) were achieved are of primary concern. Much of this information may be obtained prior to the interview from previous records and from asking parents to complete a developmental history form.

The purpose for which developmental history is used will vary. In some instances it may provide a useful clue to early problems or delays. In one case, information about a child's ear infections led to the diagnosis of chronic ear infection, a condition which, in turn, was related to the child's inattention, academic problems, and inability to get along with others. In other situations developmental history allows the evaluator to rule out certain types of problems. In all instances, however, accurate developmental information can lead to a better understanding of children.

Another frequent subject of parent interviews is parents' per-. ception of their child's personality and his or her attitude toward friends, family, school, and so forth. Interviewers are also interested in parents' description of their child's likes and dislikes, hobbies, and leisure activities. In addition, parents may be asked about their children's patterns of aggression, withdrawn behavior and other similar responses.

Of primary concern in parent interviews is a child's school history according to the parents' perception. In this connection, parents are usually asked to describe their child's school-related successes and failures, social and academic problems, as well as previous professional measures taken to diagnose or remediate home or school difficulties.

Parents' goals and expectations for their children will also be part of the interview. In this respect, the interviewer is particularly interested in differences between the expectations of parents, child, and teachers and the child's abilities. Thus, the staff of a community mental health center reported that the most significant information they gained in evaluating an out-of-control 16-year-old boy was the differences between him and his parents over plans for the teenager's future. The parents wanted their son to go to college and pursue the same profession they were in. The youth, on the other hand, was not academically inclined and was interested in following a different course after high school. Failure to resolve this difference led to a number of conflicts and eventual referral to a mental health agency for assessment of the youth.

Finally, interviewers will attempt to obtain information to aid them in better understanding a child's environment. Included will be the following: the family membership and its cultural and ethnic makeup; the economic standing of the family, including the parents' occupation; the mental and physical health of family members; languages other than English spoken by the parents or others in the family; parental child-rearing practices; and amount of supervision and contact children receive.

Again, the intent of the parent interview is to provide evaluators with a better understanding of a child's world and background. Only based on such understanding and sensitivity can a child's behavior be correctly dealt with.

Why is it important to consider physical and medical factors during evaluations?

The relationship between a person's emotional and behavioral problems and physical condition has been well documented. Problems such as malnutrition, poor health, drug/alcohol abuse and dependence, and hearing and visual disorders can contribute to emotional and behavioral problems in addition to being important considerations in the development of treatment programs. For example, one behaviorally disordered adolescent was found to have an educationally significant visual problem. The frustration of not being able to see clearly, particularly in class, caused the youngster to act-out in the classroom. Once he understood the nature of his problem and started wearing glasses the child's behavior improved dramatically.

What sorts of physical and medical factors are considered?

Professionals involved in assessing physical and medical factors will be interested in a variety of things, including:

1. frequent school absence

2. reduced physical stamina

3. frequent headaches, pains, and other physical symptoms

4. restlessness, inattention, and evidence of boredom

5. motor-control problems, including poor visual motor coordination and body balance

6. evidence of visual problems, including rubbing of eyes, excessive blinking, inflammation, and reddening of the eyes

7. evidence of hearing problems, including frequent colds or upper-respiratory infection, frequent request for repetition of directions or questions, turning one ear towards the speaker, and faulty word pronunciation

8. frequent periods of crying, excessive laughter, and other strong emotional responses, especially when a situation does not warrant such behavior

9. patterns of extreme excitability or anxiety

10. depression

11. frequent unpredictable mood shifts

12. *enuresis* (involuntary urination) or *encopresis* (soiling)

13. unkempt physical appearance

14. signs of alcohol or drug abuse or dependence

How is physical and medical information obtained?

Few educational and psychological scales are specifically designed to yield physical and medical information. Thus, much of the information obtained in the physical/medical area is based on observations (e.g., teacher or parent reports), interviews, clinical methods (e.g., examination by a physician or nurse), or tests designed to assess areas other than physical functioning (e.g., evidence of possible hearing impairment during intellectual testing).

What about assessment of perceptual-motor abilities?

In one physical-medical area—perceptual-motor skills—specific instruments are available. Moreover, because some professionals consider the development of perceptual-motor abilities an essential prerequisite to school achievement and social success percep-tual evaluation scales may be part of the evaluation. These tests are designed to determine problems in use of the senses to transmit information to the brain and to effectively use such information. Some professionals are of the opinion that percep-tual difficulties prevent children from seeing and hearing the same things as other children, thus creating social and academic problems. In order to test these skills, an array of scales may be used, most of them requiring the child to trace a maze, reproduce a geometric design or form with pencil and paper, match geometric forms, or identify partially hidden objects in a picture. In spite of the popularity of these tests, only limited validity exists for a purported significant relationship between perceptual functioning and social and academic skills. Consequently, the results of these scales should be cautiously interpreted.

How is physical and medical information used in evaluations?

Physical and medical information is often of greatest value when interpreted along with other diagnostic information. This was found to be the case in the evaluation of a 14-year-old girl. During the assessment her parents and teachers reported that she was frequently absent from school due to a variety of pains or illnesses. However, the importance of this pattern was unknown until it was learned that the teenager had recently been using alcohol to excess.

How is emotional and behavioral functioning evaluated?

The nature of emotional and behavioral evaluations varies depending on the person conducting the evaluation and the children and adolescents under study. In general, however, psychologists, educators, and other examiners use four basic methods: (a) tests; (b) observations; (c) rating scales; and (d) interviews.

What kinds of personality tests are used?

Two primary forms of tests are used in behavioral and emotional assessment: inventory scales and projective tests. *Inventory per-*

sonality scales are standardized, that is, norms have been obtained from a large number of persons, allowing evaluators to compare an individual child with other children of the same age. (The general standardization procedure described in the intelligence testing section is used.) Although most personality tests are designed for adults, a few are suitable for children and youth, including *The California Test of Personality* and the *Minnesota Multiphasic Personality Inventory* (MMPI).

How is The California Test of Personality used?

The California Test of Personality is designed for both children (from kindergarten age) and adults. Five yes-no questionnaires provide scores in two major categories: personal and social adjustment. Each of these categories is divided into six parts, giving a score based on 12 subparts. The personal and social adjustment parts include: *self-reliance, sense of personal worth, sense of freedom, feeling of belonging, withdrawing tendencies, and nervous symptoms.* The social adjustment sections consist of *social standards, social skills, antisocial tendencies, family relations, school or occupational relations,* and *community relations.*

What is the Minnesota Multiphasic Personality Inventory and how is it used?

Although the *Minnesota Multiphasic Personality Inventory* is primarily designed for adults, it is normed for adolescents 14 through 17 years old. Composed of 550 statements covering a number of personality areas, MMPI items require a "true", "false", or "cannot say" response. Examples of items include "I like mechanics magazines" and "I find it hard to keep my mind on a task or job." The scale provides information on nine clinical scales, including Depression, Schizophrenia, and Social Introversion.

What are projective tests and how are they used?

Projective tests are used primarily by clinical psychologists, but may also be used by some school psychologists and psychiatrists. These tests are not standardized. Rather, they are based on the theory that all persons, including children and adolescents, are motivated by basic psychological forces such as sexual and aggressive desires. For some children and youth these urges are so disturbing that they are blocked from consciousness. In order to understand these unconscious urges, therefore, projective techniques are used, usually in the form of ink blots and open-ended pictures which persons must interpret. Through their responses, individuals are thought to reveal their unconscious motivations and conflicts.

Projective procedures are categorized according to format. For example, association techniques require children to tell what they see when shown ink blots or to give the first word that comes to mind when presented a word by an examiner.

What types of projective tests are used with children and adolescents?

Probably the best known association technique is the *Rorschach Test*. Consisting of 10 ink blots, this test is used to assess an individual's contact with reality, motivations, adaptiveness, and other personality qualities. Like other projective instruments, the *Rorschach* consists of ambiguous stimuli which the person under evaluation supposedly interprets according to his or her personal and emotional needs. The child being tested is instructed to tell what the blots look like, what they might be, or what they make the child think of. These spontaneous responses are followed by examiner questions regarding the location of each response and the properties which evoked them.

In spite of its traditional acceptance and widespread usage, the value of the *Rorschach*, particularly with regard to school and family problems, is questionable.

What other kinds of projective tests are used with children?

Another, widely used, projective test requires children and youth to create a story after being shown a picture. The *Thematic Apperception Test* (TAT) consists of 31 drawings and photographs (e.g., a child staring at a violin). Certain items are designed for specific age and sex groups. Individuals taking the test are asked to make up a story about each drawing or photograph. Children are specifically instructed to indicate what is happening in the picture, what led up to the event, how the individuals involved felt, and how the story will turn out.

The underlying assumption of the TAT (and its counterpart, *The Children's Apperception Test*, designed for younger children) is that the stories created will reveal personality qualities and conflict situations which children are otherwise unable to understand and talk about.

How are children's responses to projective tests such as the TAT interpreted?

Interpretation of responses is based on the central figure of each story, assumed to represent the child or adolescent under study. After attempting to characterize the central figure of each story (e.g., hero—successful or frustrated), evaluators look for a general and recurring theme or situation which confronts the central character. On the basis of this information attempts are made to identify the child's personality strengths and weaknesses and his or her ways of adjusting to the world and the people who make it up.

One 8-year-old boy who had been referred because of disobedience at home and academic and conduct problems at school repeatedly responded to the TAT cards presented to him with stories about children who were afraid of being abandoned. For example, in response to one scene he noted that "The boy is wondering what he will do if his family puts him in an orphanage." These responses were considered significant in view of the divorce of the child's parents and placement of his stepbrothers and sisters with his father while he alone was assigned to live with his mother. As a result of this and other findings the child was placed in a counseling program.

Are there other ways in which projective tests are used?

Another projective assessment procedure makes use of partially completed stories or sentences for which children and adolescents must form their own conclusions. One sentence-completion procedure consists of items such as, "When I am happy I . . ."; "I get in trouble when . . ."; "It makes me angry when . . ."; and "When I grow up I want to be . . .". Particularly when combined with other information, responses such as these can provide valuable insights into personality, motivations, and conflicts.

Another projective approach requires a child to create something of his or her own choice. This expressive form of projective testing commonly involves finger painting or drawing. For example, one frequently used method requires that children draw pictures of a person. Once the drawing, assumed to represent the child, is completed the examiner asks questions about it. Personality conclusions are drawn on the basis of such information.

How are observations used in emotional/behavioral evaluations?

Behavioral observation methods, which sharply contrast with projective measures and other personality tests, are the most direct form of personality and behavioral evaluation. Direct observation makes no assumptions about the meaning of responses to artificial situations. That is, rather than attempting to determine if a child is angry and aggressive based on how he describes a picture or an ink blot, the child is directly observed in settings and at times when he might demonstrate his aggression.

This approach is based on the assumption that the environment in which an alleged problem occurs (e.g., home or school) is of crucial importance. Accordingly, when children and adolescents are evaluated using this method the evaluator goes to their home, school or other setting rather than having them come to the examiner's office.

One direct observational procedure requires that a trained observer watch a child in the classroom. Behaviors under study may include whether or not a child is attending to the assigned task and whether or not the subject is engaged in any of several improper behaviors, including hitting or touching another pupil and being out of seat without permission. Observers watch a child for set periods of time (15–20 minutes) over several days. While requiring substantial commitments from the persons conducting the evaluations, direct observation provides an effective and practical approach to understanding youngsters' problems.

How important is direct observation?

While tests and other methods of understanding children's personality and emotional makeup are important, so is direct observation. Indeed, the most efficient way of understanding children and adolescents is to watch what they do in those settings where they are alleged to be experiencing problems. Thus, a child who is of concern because he hits and kicks other children at school without provocation will probably be best understood through direct observation. For this reason parents and teachers should insist that persons conducting evaluations include in their assessment procedures direct observations.

What are rating scales and how are they used?

This form of assessment tool requires that someone familiar with a child or adolescent, usually a parent or teacher, evaluate their behavior using a structured form. Specifically, persons completing the forms are asked to rate children's behavior in comparison to other children or a hypothetical normal child. Ratings may take the form of "yes" or "no" responses or evaluations on particular dimensions (e.g., Does child fight with other children? never . . . occasionally . . . often . . . a great deal).

One popular behavioral rating scale, the teacher evaluation section of which is shown in Figure 3.2, is the Behavior Rating Profile. This rating scale allows information to be gathered from four sources: teachers, parents, peers, and the students themselves.

Behavioral ratings are used for evaluative purposes as well as treatment planning. That is, in addition to providing diagnostic personnel with an efficient and relatively easy method for evaluating a child or youth's behavior, these measures can also direct the focus of treatment. For example, if a child is consistently perceived by others as being impulsive, this problem can be made a part of the treatment.

How is interviewing used in behavioral/emotional evaluations?

Interviews are designed to yield information which facilitates accurate diagnosis and treatment. Even though the content of the interview will vary depending on the person conducting the session (e.g., psychologist, educator, or psychiatrist) and the age and problems of the child or youth under study, certain basic procedures are generally followed. Specifically, sessions will focus on many of the same areas as the parent interview. For example, children and adolescents may be asked to describe their problems, the causes of the reported difficulties, and their own feelings and those of their parents about these issues. Youngsters may also be encouraged to discuss their developmental history and personality traits, attitude toward home, school, friends, family, leisure time activities, and likes and dislikes. Special attention will probably be paid to descriptions of their relationships with peers and school personnel and their academic successes and failures. Finally, youngsters may be encouraged to discuss their personal goals, and those of their parents for them, and to describe their home and family life. In this connection, interviewers focus on differences between the responses of children and youth and those of their parents, teachers, and others. Such information will be considered in combination with other diagnostic data.

BEHAVIOR RATING PROFILE

LINDA L. BROWN & DONALD D. HAMMILL

TEACHER RATING SCALE

Student's Name: _____

Birthdate: _____

Grade: _____

Rater's Name: _____

Subject Taught: _____

School: _____

Date: _____

OTHER RELEVANT TEST SCORES:

_____

_____

_____

TEACHER'S COMMENTS AND OBSERVATION:

_____

_____

_____

_____

_____

_____

_____

_____

_____

_____

_____

_____

_____

_____

_____

_____

Raw Scores may be converted into Standard Scores and Percentile Ranks by entering the table below.

Standard Score	Raw Scores for Students in Grades 1-4	5-12	Percentile Rank
1	0-4	0-2	.1
2	5-11	3-10	.4
3	12-17	11-28	1
4	18-27	29-31	2
5	28-34	32-37	4
6	35-45	38-46	9
7	46-56	47-51	16
8	57-64	52-58	25
9	65-71	59-65	37
10	72-78	66-69	50
11	79-84	70-76	63
12	85-87	77-82	75
13	88	83-87	84
14	89	88	91
15	90	89	96
16		90	98
17			99.1
18			99.6
19			99.9
20			>99.9
M	70.6	66.2	M
SD	18.3	16.5	SD
N	387	568	N

Standard Scores: Mean = 10, Standard Deviation = 3

Results:

Raw Score _____

Standard Score _____

Percentile Rank _____

Figure 3.2. *Behavior Rating Profile.*

INSTRUCTIONS

This behavior rating form contains a list of descriptive words and phrases. Some of these items will describe the referred student quite well. Some will not. What we wish to know is this: Which of these behaviors are you concerned about at this particular time and to what extent do you see them as problems?

Take for example item #1, "Is sent to the principal for discipline." If the child frequently is sent to the principal's office, the rater might check the "Very Much Like" space. If the child is sent to the principal's office on an infrequent but regular basis, the rater might check the "Somewhat Like" space. If the child has been sent to the principal's office on rare occasions, a check in the "Not Much Like" space might be appropriate. If the child never has been disciplined by the principal, the "Not At All Like" space would be indicated. These ratings should reflect your perceptions of the child's behavior. Please do not confer with other teachers in completing this form.

The student	Very Much Like the Student	Like the Student	Not Much Like the Student	Not At All Like the Student
1. Is sent to the principal for discipline	☐	☐	☐	☐
2. Is verbally aggressive to teachers or peers	☐	☐	☐	☐
3. Is disrespectful of others' property rights	☐	☐	☐	☐
4. Tattles on classmates	☐	☐	☐	☐
5. Is lazy	☐	☐	☐	☐
6. Lacks motivation and interest	☐	☐	☐	☐
7. Disrupts the classroom	☐	☐	☐	☐
8. Argues with teachers and classmates	☐	☐	☐	☐
9. Doesn't follow directions	☐	☐	☐	☐
10. Steals	☐	☐	☐	☐
11. Has poor personal hygiene habits	☐	☐	☐	☐
12. Is passive and withdrawing	☐	☐	☐	☐
13. Says that other children don't like him/her	☐	☐	☐	☐
14. Can't seem to concentrate in class	☐	☐	☐	☐
15. Pouts, whines, snivels	☐	☐	☐	☐
16. Is overactive and restless	☐	☐	☐	☐
17. Is an academic underachiever	☐	☐	☐	☐
18. Bullies other children	☐	☐	☐	☐
19. Is self-centered	☐	☐	☐	☐
20. Does not do homework assignments	☐	☐	☐	☐
21. Is kept after school	☐	☐	☐	☐
22. Is avoided by other students in the class	☐	☐	☐	☐
23. Daydreams	☐	☐	☐	☐
24. Has unacceptable personal habits	☐	☐	☐	☐
25. Swears in class	☐	☐	☐	☐
26. Has nervous habits	☐	☐	☐	☐
27. Has no friends among classmates	☐	☐	☐	☐
28. Cheats	☐	☐	☐	☐
29. Lies to avoid punishment or responsibility	☐	☐	☐	☐
30. Doesn't follow class rules	☐	☐	☐	☐

Sum of Marks in Each Column = _____

Multiply Sum by   X 0   X 1   X 2   X 3

Add Products   0 + _____ + _____ + _____ = _____

Total Points Scored

Figure 3.2. *Continued.*

Why is it important to consider academic abilities as a part of assessment?

Differences between children's or adolescents' intellectual abilities and their academic achievement rank among the best indicators of significant behavioral or emotional problems. Further, since school-age emotionally and behaviorally disturbed youngsters almost always have significant academic problems, these difficulties must be identified and understood so that suitable remediation programs can be planned. Assessment of academic skills and abilities, therefore, must be a part of the overall evaluation, including classroom records and grades, and results of group tests and individualized academic measures (e.g., reading, math, spelling, language).

Summary

Assessment is a significant part of meeting the needs of behaviorally disordered and emotionally disturbed children and adolescents. Even though personality and overall mental health is complex and difficult to evaluate, suitable and reasonably effective tests and procedures are available for this purpose. With skillful application of such methods children and adolescents requiring professional attention can be identified and receive appropriate treatment.

What Are the Major Forms of Emotional and Behavioral Problems?

4

 The purpose of this chapter is to answer some of the questions that revolve around the various labels attached to children and youth who have emotional and behavioral problems. The reader should be cautioned not to make hasty generalizations about people who may possess *some* of these characteristics. Emotional and behavioral disorders are described in very general terms to acquaint the reader with the terminology. Attention should be given to children and youth who are very different from what is considered normal. This chapter is intended to demystify some of the often confusing labels that are being commonly used.

Conduct Disorders

My son supposedly has a conduct disorder. What is that?

A *conduct disorder* is a behavior that prevents the child, or other children, from learning and behaving appropriately. Examples of conduct disorders include:

Out of seat often

Constantly talks to others or self

Makes noises

Doesn't pay attention to task(s)

Ignores classroom rules

Refuses to work

Disobedient to teacher

Physically bothers students

Fights with others

Persistently lying

Blames others

Truant

If your son exhibits one or more of these behaviors often, he may be described as having a conduct disorder.

What causes conduct disorders?

Many things. Frustration with school work, boredom with assignments, insecurity among friends, need for attention, or perhaps problems outside the classroom such as the bus, playground or home. Chapter 2 explains more fully what can contribute to conduct disorders.

The teacher says that Gary stares out the window much of the time. How is this a conduct disorder?

Gary's teacher believes that the constant staring is getting in the way of his learning. His conduct, therefore, is interfering with him getting the information that his teacher feels is necessary for him to achieve in the classroom.

Frankie has always been a fidgety child. He rocks, taps his fingers, or does other things that drives me crazy. His teachers call this "self-stimulation." What does that mean?

Self-stimulatory behaviors are behaviors that are repetitive and frequent. They do not cause physical injury to self and/or others. Examples of these behaviors are:

finger waggling

finger tapping

body motions such as rocking, swaying

and in more severe instances:

screaming

saying the same words or phrases repeatedly

masturbation

In some instances students may behave in self-stimulatory ways, such as rocking, but their learning is not affected. The teacher, however, may be disturbed by the behavior, or might be concerned about the social inappropriateness of such behavior. This is an instance where referral or remediation will depend on the judgment of the teacher(s). Certainly, a teacher's tolerance of these behaviors is an important factor.

Tolerance? A teacher's tolerance may decide if my child is going to get help? Or be labeled?

There is little doubt that individuals have different tolerances for certain behaviors. For example, there are most likely things the readers would accept as tolerable but that their best friend would not tolerate. Sometimes, teachers are not perceived as having the right to be (in)tolerant of certain behaviors.

Some teachers may not mind it if students talk quietly among themselves, get up often to do minor tasks, tap quietly on their desks, or occasionally look out the window. Other teachers believe such behaviors are unacceptable. They might set up a very strict classroom rule system whereby the occurrence of the above behaviors result in immediate negative consequences. Clearly, students who violate the rules, for whatever reason, will be punished.

It is important to remember that different teachers have different levels of tolerance. While it would obviously be preferable that teachers are always the same, it would be unrealistic to expect them to behave that way all the time.

Is it possible for my child to be conduct disordered at school and not at home?

Yes. Many tasks at school differ from those at home. For example, at home and in the community, children and youth are not usually required to respond to such academic tasks as reading and mathematics. Since these activities are not a regular part of their homelife, children may find it difficult to adjust in school. At home, on the other hand, where many activities involve behaviors that require children to actively do something, such as chores, children may be compliant and show little frustration.

Further, some children may be accustomed to a great deal of attention at home. When teachers have class sizes of 25 to 35 students, children may receive less attention than they do at home. This may lead to attention-getting behaviors on the part of some. If the child can perform school activities well, the attention received will most likely be positive. If, however, schoolwork is too difficult and becomes frustrating, students may behave in a manner that draws negative attention.

Discipline may represent another area of differences between home and school. For example, parents may use physical punishment as a means to insure obedience whereas the teacher may simply yell or send students out of the room. For these students yelling does not invoke the same fear as being punished. Far from being a plea for use of corporal punishment in the schools, this observation points to the realization that differences in types of management between school and home may result in different levels of compliance to rules and consequences.

School requires children to interact and also function in groups. For the most part, these are behaviors that children bring to school from home. Many students have not had many opportunities to interact with others for such a large part of the day. The inability of some to respect the rights and property of others might lead to classroom problems.

Hyperactivity

Are conduct disorders, attention deficit disorders, and "hyperactivity" the same things?

"My child cannot sit down for more than a minute! Even when he's sitting, his legs are swinging, his hands are moving, or he's rocking his whole body. He just won't sit still!"

"Tim is so easily frustrated. Last week he was playing with his truck, and when the wheel fell off, he threw the truck at his sister. She had to get three stitches!"

One way to describe *hyperactivity* (also known as *attention deficit disorders*) is to look at the word itself. "Hyper" means excessive or too much. Hyperactivity is just that, too much of a particular activity (or behavior). In both of the preceding cases, the children reacted with too much activity. Hyperactivity refers to behaviors which occur too often or too quickly and are inappropriate for particular settings. In school, hyperactivity interferes with learning and causes academic and social problems.

Hyperactivity is often used to describe the behavior problems of learning disabled students because of their inability to complete their work successfully. Also, it has been suggested that hyperactivity may be due to biophysical problems. Some common behaviors associated with hyperactivity are:

stubborn—"She absolutely refuses to do anything that I ask!"

negative—"He never allows himself to have a good time. She thinks that nobody likes her."

impulsive—"He doesn't think before he acts. He just acts!"

temper outbursts—"Anytime she has any difficulty, she screams and acts crazy!"

inattentive—"He doesn't concentrate . . . doesn't seem to listen."

bossy—"She always has to be in charge. She gets upset when she doesn't have her way."

low frustration tolerance—"The slightest problem becomes a major catastrophe to him."

lack of response—"It doesn't matter what I do. Nothing seems to get through!"

motor activity—"He can't be still. He is always moving around, even when he is in bed."

Hyperactivity is usually described as a chronic condition. That is, hyperactivity describes behaviors that occur almost constantly. The term may be used incorrectly to describe children's behavior during certain special events, such as parties, trips, or group gatherings.

Does that mean that when Bobby hits people if he doesn't get his way, he has hyperactivity?

It is not important to categorize physical aggression. Physical aggression may or may not be due to hyperactivity. What *is* important is that physical aggression is inappropriate both at home and in school.

Aggressive Behaviors

What exactly is "aggression"?

Aggression is another term that also has different meanings to different people. The authors prefer to designate aggression as behavior that severely interferes with others. In other words, aggression can be seen when a child is upset and then becomes abusive to others or to objects in the environment.

Aggression can take many forms. Some milder, and sometimes accepted, examples of aggression include:

teasing

clowning around

bullying

tattling

having temper tantrums

threats of aggression

Once again, teachers may react differently to these behaviors. To some people, the above examples are not considered very serious and are tolerated. Other and more severe aggressive acts include:

threats of physical aggression

physical attacks on people

destruction of property

cruelty to animals

What is the difference between aggression and temper tantrums?

A child having a temper tantrum, although disturbing, usually poses no threat to self, others or property. Aggression, on the other hand, poses such a threat. With both aggression and temper tantrums, the child may be considered to be out of control. Both emotions may be due to an inability to cope with frustration. In many cases, temper tantrums can be ignored, which might, in turn, lower their frequency. Aggression cannot be ignored because of its severity, not to mention the rights of potential victims.

Temper tantrums, as well as other examples of mild aggression, may be tolerated by some. However, such behavior clearly interferes with learning. Further, temper tantrums may lead to aggression if left unchecked. For example, an otherwise unaggressive student or sibling might be provoked enough by constant teasing to physically retaliate.

Anxiety

My child is always worrying. She doesn't sleep well nor does she do well on her schoolwork because she is too afraid that she won't do well. What's her problem?

It sounds like your daughter might have what is called *anxiety*. Anxiety means fear of the unknown. Individuals suffering from anxiety perceive events as very threatening, even though they might prove to be nonthreatening or at the most, unpleasant. Anxious people tend to work themselves into such a state that they are unable to achieve at their level of competence. For example:

> "Sue is a good student, yet, she frets so much. She worries about everything. She worries about school, about having friends, about how she looks. You name it, she worries about it. Even when things work out for her, she goes on to worry about the next thing. She is impossible to be around during these times."

Sue has an anxiety disorder. She worries excessively over a wide range of areas, including academics and social acceptance. It is not unusual for people such as Sue to experience severe anxiety (or be anxious) about such things as:

possible injuries or illnesses

the ability to live up to the expectations of others

taking field trips with a school group

talking to others

Each of these examples may give rise to concern or mild anxiety in most people, but they usually are able to complete their task despite their concern. The anxious individual in contrast, is overly concerned and may not be able to attempt or, possibly, complete a task.

Fred becomes hysterical when I leave him in kindergarten, or even if I leave him at a friend's house when I do a short errand. Is this anxiety?

Yes, this is a problem that is sometimes called *separation anxiety*. Separation anxiety refers to a specific type of fear, namely, the fear that a loved one or significant other will not return. Such anxiety is intense, sometimes approaching panic. Some children may develop problems going to sleep, and when they do, they might have nightmares.

Billy is a good kid. He has friends, has gone to camp; yet, he refuses to go to school. He starts to hyperventilate when he sees the school bus. Is this separation anxiety?

Once again, it is difficult to be sure of a particular diagnosis, especially because so little information is available. If parents or others are concerned about children who seem to experience the emotions and behaviors described in this chapter, a complete diagnosis may be in order.

It might be that Billy has a school phobia. The term *phobia* is rarely used in educational circles, more often it is discussed by psychologists or psychiatrists. Phobias are intense fears of specific objects or events that pose little or no threat to the individual.

A school phobia is refusal to attend school because the child is unusually afraid of the school and the school environment. This differs from separation anxiety, where the child is afraid to go anywhere if it means being apart from the parents.

Phobias

**Jenny is afraid of the neighbor's dog,
even though it is on a chain.
Jenny goes out of her way to avoid the dog.
Is this a phobia?**

Maybe, but probably not. Most likely, Jenny is experiencing a rather normal childhood fear. People, and especially children, are afraid of all sorts of things, for example, darkness and animals. It is only when this fear is so overwhelming that it becomes debilitating and significantly interferes with the child's functioning that it is considered to be a phobia. If Jenny was afraid to go to sleep, to leave the house, or participate in various activities because of the dog, she would have a phobia (or be phobic) about the dog.

Depression

**I know this might be a dumb question,
but can my 8-year-old be suffering from depression?
Barry lies around the house all the time.
He doesn't want to do anything.
He goes to school, but he just sits
there and does very little.**

Historically, it was believed that children couldn't be depressed based on the notion that there simply wasn't anything an 8-year-old child could be depressed about. However, depression is evident in some children and youth in our schools. It is one of the most difficult forms of emotional disturbance or behavioral disorder to diagnose.

In a large regular education classroom setting, depressed students can be overlooked. Teachers have difficulty enough teaching those students who are not attending to their schoolwork. These students are usually easy to identify because of behaviors that disturb the teacher or fellow students. Depressed children, in contrast, are rarely disturbing to others. They are sometimes categorized as being turned-off by school, rather than as being emotionally disturbed.

Identifying depressed children and youth usually requires understanding their history. In other words, is their current behavior markedly different from their previous behavior? Behavior changes can serve as warning signals of depression. Many times they are coupled with general feelings of sadness. Contrary to popular belief, an exhibition of sadness does not always accompany depression. Unexplained and many times significant behavior changes that may signify depression include:

crying

withdrawal from friends

disinterest in school

physical complaints

change in sleeping habits (too much or too little sleep)

change in eating habits (too much or too little)

lack of bladder control

reduced physical activity

apathy

drug or alcohol abuse

delinquency

What would cause a child to get depressed?

Children and youth face problems that they perceive to be as catastrophic as any an adult may face. In fact, some people believe that depression may be learned. Children may be modeling the reactions, as they perceive them, that their parents exhibit to unfortunate events.

Traumatic events that may trigger depression in children include:

death of a significant other (parent, sibling)

divorce of parents

family stresses (money, relationship problems)

It would be incorrect to suggest that it is these events alone that cause depression. People have their own way of perceiving events. The depressed child looks at events in a much more negative, helpless, and, perhaps hopeless manner than others.

Juvenile Delinquency

My son's teacher called him a juvenile delinquent because he gets into so much trouble at school. Does that make him a juvenile delinquent?

No, the term *juvenile delinquent* a is legal one; however, it has been applied to youth who are troublesome. In most states, juvenile delinquents are those under the age of 18 who have been found guilty of an illegal act by a court. Crimes may include acts for which adults would not be arrested such as truancy, running away from home, and incorrigibility.

What is a "socialized" delinquent?

A *socialized delinquent* is a child or youth who, for all intents and purposes, is normal, yet, highly influenced by peers. A common trait of a socialized delinquent is membership in a youth gang or club.

Do all delinquents join clubs and gangs?

No. Some delinquents have no friends. They may seem irritable, aggressive, defiant, quarrelsome, and unmotivated by praise or punishment.

Another type of delinquent are children who tend to be unhappy. In contrast to the delinquents just described, these children and youth experience genuine remorse and anxiety over their behaviors. Many of them are withdrawn and sometimes seem shy. While these delinquents generally do not repeat their acts, their disorders can be very serious. For these children and adolescents, the delinquency seems to be a secondary problem that has resulted from their emotional problems.

Is a child with a learning disability more prone to become a delinquent?

Some young people with learning disabilities (any inability to understand spoken or written language) may exhibit delinquent behaviors if their frustrations with their disabilities are not dealt with at home or at school.

There are many theories of delinquency ranging from the sociological to the behavioral to the psychological. Again, causation should not be the major concern. Rather, both parents and educators should focus on remediation.

Substance Abuse

Is depression temporary or can it lead to other problems such as drug and alcohol abuse?

If children or youth are experiencing depression and do not receive proper attention by those around them, other problems can arise. By definition, those who exhibit behaviors that are indicative of depression are rarely disturbing. If, however, a significant change in behavior occurs, even one that does not bother others, parents and teachers should try to determine the cause and help the individual. Alcohol and drug abuse often is the result of emotional problems such as depression.

Studies have shown that many depressed adolescents turn to drugs because of reported:

low self-concept

need to escape

boredom

peer pressure

enjoyment

Many children experiment with substances such as marijuana, alcohol, valium, quaaludes, cocaine, and glue, to name a few. Drug users display a variety of symptoms related to each specific drug. However, common symptoms are:

sleepiness

slurring of speech

incoherent, confused state

mood swings

blood-shot eyes

When does drinking alcohol become a problem? I know my daughter drinks.

As with all the forms of emotional disturbance and behavioral disorders that have been discussed, substance intake is a problem when it calls attention to itself. Consider the following:

"I take a drink in the morning, just to . . . you know . . . get it going. Facing mom and dad is such a hassle. A little vodka just takes the edge off . . . you know? I keep my old Flintstones thermos in my locker at school. No one would ever look in there. I keep vodka or whiskey. Whichever is easier to get. Sometimes I steal it from my parents. They'd never guess . . . you know?

School's such a drag. Although, sometimes I get really tired in school. When I go home, I go up to my room to drink. Who cares? At least I'm not popping pills like my friends. I use a little breath spray to cover up while I eat dinner. Then I really get blitzed until I can't feel anything anymore. What's the big deal? Everybody drinks . . . you know? I might stop when I'm 14 though. Who knows?"

Alcoholics and other substance abusers usually need intake at least daily. The need for the substance often becomes physiological (the body becomes addicted) as well as psychological.

Alcoholics may have regularly defined drinking periods, such as weekends and/or they may binge. A binge is when the individual undergoes periods of sobriety interspersed with periods of heavy intake that may last days, weeks, or months.

Alcohol is a socially accepted substance and is easy to obtain. It is also the most commonly abused. Whatever the substance, it may not be long before the major goal of the child's day (and, perhaps life) is to obtain the substance.

Withdrawn Behaviors

My daughter has been described as ''withdrawn.'' Is that the same as depression?

No, except for some cases where withdrawn behaviors are the result of depression. Some children and youth exhibit withdrawn behaviors without being depressed. Consider, the following vignette:

> "Susan is in the fifth grade. She never causes trouble and is very quiet. She will answer questions, but does not initiate conversations with anyone. She doesn't have any friends. The kids in class tease her, but she doesn't seem to mind. She just goes off to be by herself."

Withdrawal is one way students may escape unpleasant situations. It may result from lack of social skills required in certain situations. That is, children may not know how to behave in social groups or in classroom situations. They may have experienced rejection or humiliation in those groups and have learned that it is better not to associate with others than risk failing again. Some typical withdrawn behaviors include:

avoidance of eye contact

avoidance of association with peers

seeming embarrassment

refusal to participate in group discussions

physical isolation

playing mostly with inanimate objects

Susan isn't disrupting the class, and she is still learning in her class. Why, then, is her teacher concerned?

Clearly, Susan poses no immediate problems in the classroom. However, if she is not taught to understand her situation and deal with it, more severe mental health problems may develop. Susan's type of social withdrawal may delay normal social development, and if it lasts into her high school years, where interrelationships take on added importance, it could also hamper her ability to achieve.

Anorexia Nervosa

What is this disease that people talk about so much . . . anorexia nervosa?

Anorexia nervosa is an intense fear, usually prevalent in girls, of being or becoming obese. The person's self-image is very distorted. Anorectics may be extremely underweight, and yet believe they are overweight. The adolescent or young adult with anorexia nervosa experiences a severe weight loss that, in turn, causes many other physical problems. Anorectics believe that their perceptions of being overweight are accurate. To complicate matters, the anorectic is not disturbing to others. Consider the following example:

"Our Cathy is such a good girl. She never caused us trouble. In fact, sometimes we think she pushes herself too hard. She gets all As, is active in cheerleading, and our church. She studies hard and keeps her room as neat as a pin.

We still feel that something is wrong. She is so skinny. She sits with us at dinner, but seems to just play with her food. Last night, my husband forced her to eat. A little while later, I was on my way upstairs when I heard her vomiting. When I went into the bathroom, she had her fingers down her throat.

I confronted her and she told me that she was under control. She broke down and said that she was too fat. She looks like she is starving and she says that she is too fat."

What do I look for if I suspect anorexia?

As with the many other problems that have been discussed in this chapter, the following symptoms are meant to be warning signals. That is, they *might* indicate anorexia nervosa.

A preoccupied fear of obesity

An inability to logically view the body . . . a fear of being fat though emaciated—Sally stands in front of the mirror and her bones stick out, yet, she cries that she can still pull skin away from her body

An inability to maintain body weight because of vomiting, strenuous exercise, intake of huge amounts of laxatives, strict refusal to eat

Excessive weight loss, at least 25% body weight

No known physical illness that accounts for weight loss

Obsessive, ritualistic behaviors—"Her clothes and shoes are in perfect order, she places silverware and dishes in a specific way, and I think she even chews her food a certain number of times and in a certain way!"

What causes anorexia nervosa?

There is no known cause of anorexia. While it is largely viewed as a psychological problem that can cause physical problems, some recent evidence suggests that it might be due to the individual's metabolism.

Bulimia

My child will sit down and eat everything in sight. Yet, she isn't gaining any weight. Yesterday I found boxes of laxatives in her drawer. Does she have anorexia?

Maybe, although it sounds like she may have a related eating disorder: bulimia. Bulimia is exhibited by frequent episodes of uncontrollable eating—when a person consumes vast amounts of food within a short period of time. The person feels unable to stop eating, called a "binge." Bulimics alternate binging with self-induced vomiting or extreme laxative use, called "purging." Purging rids the body of the large amounts of food eaten.

What is the difference between bulimia and anorexia?

Bulimics are able to view what they are doing as being abnormal, but they cannot control or stop the behavior. Anorectics do not view their behavior as abnormal.

Enuresis

Bobby wets himself all the time, day and night. Does he have an emotional problem?

Bobby may have enuresis, which is the involuntary voiding of urine that is *not* due to physical problems. Many professionals believe enuresis may be a symptom of underlying stress or a problem the child is experiencing. The condition may also be due to delayed or incomplete toilet training.

Some recent research has centered around the intensity of sleep of children with enuresis to test the theory that some children sleep so deeply that they fail to respond to the sensation of a full bladder.

Encopresis

Jimmy soils himself. Is this the same as enuresis?

No, voluntary or involuntary passage of feces in inappropriate places is called *encopresis.* Involuntary soiling applies to children who soil themselves when a problem such as severe constipation is present, while voluntary means that the soiling is deliberate. Like enuresis, the condition is usually diagnosed after all organic or physical causes have been ruled out. As for enuresis, the causes usually are due to stress or underlying problems.

You mention that organic or physical problems must be ruled out before enuresis or encopresis can be determined. Aren't these physical problems to begin with?

Yes, however, these physical problems may be the result of an emotional problem. Other physical problems may result from emotional problems. Some of these will be briefly discussed below. If your child has one of these problems, it does not necessarily mean that it is accompanied by an emotional problem, however. Some physical problems that may have a relationship to emotional problems include:

Childhood asthma—severe difficulties breathing (coughing, shortness of breath) resulting from infections, allergies, or stress

Ulcerative colitis—disorder of the gastrointestinal system resulting in severe diarrhea, abdominal pains, and damage to the intestinal lining

Elective mutism—child virtually refuses to speak in certain situations or chooses only to speak to specific people. Most commonly, the child refuses to speak in school, to strangers, or in other stressful situations

Obesity—defined as body weight that is 20% or greater than the norm for the height and weight of the child. An obese child is one who may use food as a substitute for affection and social attention or as a release from stress. Many obese children have few friends and find school traumatic. They may appear to be dependent and immature; yet, in many cases, they are demanding with their parents.

Autism

My son flaps his hands, screams at a very high pitch and runs back and forth on his tiptoes for hours. Nothing seems to matter to him. Is this autism? What is autism?

Your son may have autism, or he may have autistic-like behaviors and be severely handicapped in another way. The remainder of this chapter will discuss some forms of autism and severe emotional disturbance. Autism is a lifelong disability. Its symptoms interfere with a child's ability to communicate his or her needs, to socially interact with people, and to learn. Autism is sometimes apparent when the child is a baby, but is not usually diagnosed until 2 or 3 years of age.

Aren't autism and emotional disturbance the same?

No. Many professionals once believed that autism was a result of an emotional trauma, or perhaps an incomplete relationship with a parent. There is no evidence to suggest that there is any validity to this theory, however. Many emotionally healthy families have an autistic member.

What are the symptoms of autism?

> Our son's supposed or possible hearing problem became more compounded by his tendency to stare and be passive. When we picked him up, his arms casually dangled at his sides as if they were disconnected from his body. He expressed dislike or discomfort with physical contact by pushing our hands away when we tried to embrace him. He consistently chose one or two toys or objects to play with and would often go off by himself. [1]

Kaufman is describing *his* autistic son's characteristics. Other children may exhibit behaviors such as the following:

Displays odd mannerisms. The child exhibits hand flicking, staring, rocking, running on tiptoes.

Difficulty mixing with other children. Prefers to play by themselves

Seems to be "deaf." One minute the child shows no reaction to loud noises, the next minute the child reacts to a noise in the next room

---

[1] Kaufman, B. N. (1976). *Son rise*. New York: Harper & Row.

Not responsive to human contact

Does not make eye contact

Marked physical activity

Might spin objects or display inappropriate attachment to objects. The child will sit and spin dishes, wheels, flick toys over and over, etc.

No fear of real dangers

Resists change in routine

Does not orally communicate needs, might communicate needs by gesturing

I think my child has this last characteristic. All she does is repeat what I say. If I ask Joy if she wants a cookie, all she will say is the same thing back to me: "Want a cookie. Do you want a cookie, etc."

You are describing one of the most frustrating characteristics of an autistic child: problems in communicating. Repeating words or phrases is called *echolalia*; it is very common among children with autism.

Gesturing at objects instead of using words is also very common. Speech is sometimes nonexistent. The same child, however, may respond to directions or commands. For example, the child can comply with "Come here" or "Sit down" as well as two-step directions such as "Go get your coat and put it on."

Betty can't seem to do things other children can do and yet she is the same age. Is she mentally retarded?

The symptoms of autism interfere with the child's ability to learn. If the child prefers to sit and rock, or constantly spin an object, he or she is difficult to teach. Because the symptoms get in the way of learning, autistic children function at a much lower level than their peers, thus appearing to be mentally retarded.

How could this happen to my child? What did I do wrong?

"I wasn't prepared for Brian. I just had Steve. Two children under 2 years old seemed impossible to me. I wasn't happy being pregnant, but I loved him once he was here. Could this be my fault?"

"I thought Gene was a good baby. He never cried or fussed. He just sat in the crib and rocked. I should have stopped him. I was busy and he seemed happy. I should have stopped him and then he wouldn't be autistic."

Autism is not anyone's fault. It is believed to be caused by a physical problem. Neurological problems and chemical imbalances in the human body are currently being studied as possible causes. Autism is present at birth. It has nothing to do with what parents did or didn't do. Autism affects all races, all economic levels, and both girls and boys.

I have heard that autistic children are violent. Will my child be violent? What will happen to my child?

Nobody can predict whether an autistic child will become aggressive. It is a problem of some autistic children, but certainly not most. Each child is an individual and should be treated as such. And, because each child's needs are different, so are the options for treatment that are open to a parent.

Childhood Schizophrenia

Is autism the same as schizophrenia?

Schizophrenia refers to a group of disorders that cause disturbances in thinking, moods, and behavior. These disturbances are basically misinterpretations of reality. For example, schizophrenic children may have speech ability, yet, their speech will have no meaning to others.

Disturbances in mood involve inappropriate emotional responses. Examples of this might include laughing when someone is seriously hurt or crying over cartoons. Disturbances in behaviors might be total withdrawal or exhibiting bizarre behaviors.

What are bizarre behaviors?

Bizarre behaviors are highly unusual; they may be fascinating to the observer or extremely frustrating. Consider the behaviors of the following children:

> "My son is fascinated with elevators. When we travel anywhere, he runs to find an elevator. Once he finds one, he will question for hours whether it has a gate or door and whether it's operated by hand or buttons. He never stops asking the same questions."

> "Sam was such a good baby. However, he seems to be so preoccupied with things. At five, we had to constantly watch him because he would collect everyone's doormats in the neighborhood. He loved doormats."

Other examples of the bizarre behaviors that autistic and/or schizophrenic children may exhibit include:

Delayed or incoherent speech—I ask him if he's hungry and he asks me if the elevator is running."

Disordered thought process—"Although completely toilet trained, Jerry became anxious and confused if he had to urinate and have a bowel movement at the same time. He would run to an adult and ask if he was a boy or a girl. His reasoning was that a boy urinates standing up, a girl sitting down. Therefore, if he sat down for a bowel movement and urinated at the same time, he might be a girl"[2].

Displaying a constant desire to be alone

Preoccupation with objects, displaying compulsive rituals—"He has to circle the table exactly twenty-two times before sitting down to eat."

Extreme hyperactivity

What is the cause of schizophrenia?

"My wife never said as much, but I'm sure that she resented my schooling, while she stayed home with Sam. Could her resentment have caused this?"

"My husband was never home. He worked constantly. When he was home, he wanted to sleep. I know he loves Jim, but he never seemed to have any time for him."

At this time, there is no one single known cause of schizophrenia. Certainly, it is not necessarily caused by the actions of parents. Instead, there is a widespread belief that genetic vulnerability may be an underlying factor. *Genetic vulnerability* means that if a grandfather, for example, is an adult schizophrenic, the chances increase for a child or grandchild to become schizophrenic more than somebody who has no schizophrenia in the family. This does not mean that it will definitely occur, it only means that the chances are greater.

It is also generally accepted that childhood schizophrenia is associated with chemical imbalances. Such factors as enzyme

---

[2] Davids, A. (1974). *Children in conflict: A casebook.* New York: Wiley.

levels and metabolisms are being studied to determine their contribution to this illness.

Summary

When parents are faced with a troubled child or adolescent, they may be overwhelmed with the labels or terms used to describe their child. This chapter has provided brief descriptions of a number of emotional and behavioral disorders. Hopefully, the information will serve as a point from which the reader can begin to understand these otherwise often confusing terms.

Where Can My Child Get Help?

 It is important to understand that it is difficult to predict how any *one* school district will act to help emotionally disturbed and behaviorally disordered students. While laws have been developed to guide the educational system, some schools, for reasons that will be discussed later, circumvent or bend the rules. The purpose of this chapter is to answer questions that are often asked in connection with the public education of students with emotional or behavioral problems.

What happens after my child has been diagnosed as having emotional or behavioral problems?

This is a very important question and it involves a process that is as significant as diagnosis and assessment. The ways students are identified as having emotional and/or behavioral problems were explained in Chapter 3. Professional evaluations and their purpose were discussed to help the reader understand this complicated and, oftentimes, confusing procedure. Identification of the child, however, is only half of the process.

What do you mean "half"? I thought identification naturally leads to placement in a special education class.

Not necessarily. Placement may be handled differently from school district to school district. However, all placements should be guided by the spirit of the *least restrictive environment* philosophy stated in the Education for All Handicapped Children (EHA) federal law. The least restrictive environment, however, can be interpreted differently. And, like other professionals, the authors of this book have their own view of what they believe insures the best possible education for special education students.

Isn't the "least restrictive environment" the same as mainstreaming students from special education settings into the regular education classroom?

No. Although *mainstreaming* also can have many meanings, the most common definition of the term suggests that handicapped students are best placed in a regular education setting. For now, let's avoid the term mainstreaming and concentrate on the least restrictive environment, which can be defined as the setting in which a student's handicap does not interfere with, or get in the way of his or her learning.

For example, the least restrictive environment for severely emotionally disturbed students who do not have the ability to control their behaviors might be a very structured setting such as a residential or day school that is separate from the public school. (Later in this chapter, the functions of the many types of placements will be discussed.)

Rarely are severely disturbed students placed in the regular classroom because the teacher most likely will not have the time nor the necessary skills to teach them. The academic curriculum for severely disturbed students tends to be on a significantly lower level than that of the other students. With the large number of regular education students in many regular education classrooms, teachers usually teach to the majority of the students, leaving less instructional time for the special education students.

Further, it is possible that the regular education teacher has not been trained to meet the special needs of severely emotionally disturbed students. Finally, these students may have a disturbing influence on other students, by exhibiting behaviors that normally lead to such disciplinary actions as exclusion from class, detention, and suspension, all resulting in less teaching time for all students. Therefore, the regular education classroom is usually not the *least restrictive environment* for most severely disturbed students. In fact, it is a setting that can be *very* restrictive to such students' academic and behavioral growth.

How is the least restrictive environment determined for my child?

The least restrictive environment for special education students is determined through careful examination of the student's needs and selection of the program that most effectively helps meet these needs. A rather complex issue sometimes arises in this connection when parents want the very *best* program for their child. This goal is desirable for all students; however, under the least restrictive environment concept, schools are only required to place students in a setting where their handicap will not interfere with learning.

Placements, hopefully, are dictated by students' needs. In other words, assessment information, both formal and informal, should determine what programs *and placements* are needed so that students are not handicapped in their educational pursuits.

What placements are available in schools and how do they differ from each other?

School district placement options are associated with many factors. The size of the school system, its location, relative wealth, and its commitment to education each has an impact on the quality and quantity of available placement choices. Generally, placement options fall within the following continuum, although some school districts may not offer all of them.

The Regular Education Classroom

The regular education setting is often perceived as the "least restrictive". Placement in this setting suggests that the student may not receive any special services (e.g., counseling). If the student has special needs, it is the regular education teacher's responsibility to meet those needs.

Consequently, if a student is placed in a regular education classroom, he or she should be able to function with little special assistance. Since regular education teachers are responsible for teaching 20 to 35 students, it is unrealistic to expect that much of their time can be devoted to one or two handicapped students. In other words, handicapped students placed in a regular education setting should be capable of being taught in *basically* the same way as other students. By definition, handicapped students are placed in the program by which they are best served—academically, socially, emotionally, and behaviorally.

Regular Education Classroom with Consultation

This placement is only slightly different from the previous setting. Students are assigned to regular class settings on a full-time basis; however, specialists are available for consultation with the teacher or parent(s). Consultants may offer specific techniques or general programs to help remediate the students' problem.

This placement, as with the others, has a very important reality component. Thus, it is important to determine if appropriate consultation services are available before it is recommended for a particular student. Also, does the regular education teacher have time during the day to receive the consultation? And, does the consultant have a case load that will realistically allow for consulting?

Consultation with Direct Services

As with the previous two placement options, students are assigned to regular education settings on a full-time basis with specialists available to the teacher and parent. Additionally, short-term direct services may be provided to help the student handle the regular education routine.

Direct services may include help in a particular academic or skill area. Recess, lunch room, or physical education assistance, as well as the traditional kinds of academic and behavioral assistance, may be included with this placement.

Resource Room

Students assigned to resource rooms spend most of the school day in the regular classroom; however, they receive services in a special education classroom for as much as three hours per day. Resource rooms may serve students with varying mild handicaps, of different ages, grades, and ability. Implementation of this program option also differs from district to district as well as being influenced by the type of school (e.g., elementary, middle, secondary).

Resource rooms may also differ according to the philosophies of the teachers. For example, many resource rooms function as a supplement to regular education classrooms. Special education teachers, with consultation from regular educators, arrange the students' program so they can stay in the regular setting as much as possible, and still have their needs met in those subjects with which they encounter most difficulty. The special education teachers might tutor the students in particular subjects (most common in the upper grades) or teach them those skills that allow them to compete in the regular education setting, for example, reading.

The problem with this philosophy is that the resource room may be filled with many students, each having his or her specific problems. In other words, there might be three students from each grade in the resource room at the same time, each for a different reason (e.g., reading, math, or social skills training). The resource room teacher has the difficult task of consulting with all the students' teachers *and* teaching each student within a very narrow timeframe.

Critics of the resource room concept claim that it is difficult for one teacher to meet all students' needs, even with the help of an aide. Thus, to be able to manage a resource room, special education teachers may have to resort to a large amount of seatwork, leaving little time for teaching. Seatwork often takes the form of dittos and workbooks resulting in little motivation to learn on the part of the students. Yet, teachers in these programs may have little choice of teaching style since it would be virtually impossible for them to *teach* each student individually.

Not all resource rooms present such a bleak picture. In some schools, especially in the upper grades, teachers teach the same subject matter to the entire class (e.g., reading, social studies) and individualize instruction based on students' learning styles. This is much more manageable and effective than trying to teach everybody everything at once.

Part-Time Special Class

Students in this setting attend a special education classroom for most of the day, and are integrated into regular education settings for a few class periods. Many times the classes the students attend with their nonhandicapped peers are "specials," such as industrial education, art, music, and physical education.

Parents and professionals should be cautioned not to place students in classes that are designated as specials simply because they are not traditionally academic in nature. Some of these "specials" require skills that some students have not been able to demonstrate in other settings, such as the inability to control frustration, which may result in tools being broken or thrown, or the inability to read, which may result in failing music. In fact, many of these "specials" provide less structure than many regular education classrooooms. For example, behavioral expectations in an art class or wood shop area are often more relaxed, or at least more independent, than the regular class. These different expectations may give rise to more problems for both students and their teachers.

Not all school systems call this setting "part-time." Students attending this type of program might simply be classified as attending special education, or a resource room, or a self-contained class (discussed below), with some provision allowed for attending regular classes.

Full-Time or Self-Contained Special Class

Students in this setting are in public special classes for the entire day, with the possible exceptions of lunch, recess, and physical education. This is the most restrictive of the settings listed thus far. Yet, it is not too restrictive for students requiring a highly structured program.

Sometimes, people perceive self-contained special class settings as negative. Because of their restrictiveness self-contained classrooms are chosen with some hesitation. Hopefully, students who are placed in such settings are those who will benefit the most from it, and who have demonstrated that their handicap(s) have prevented them from learning in less restrictive settings. Placing students in an inappropriate placement because it seems more normal does not take into consideration the feelings of insecurity and frustration that students experience when they cannot learn or behave in the manner expected of them.

Public or Private Day School

If the students' behavior cannot be managed and/or remediated in a regular education setting, placement outside a traditional public school may be necessary. There are a variety of options from which to choose, and in addition to selecting the program that best meets a student's needs, accessibility is an important consideration, that is, distance from the home and cost.

Day schools may take the form of alternative schools, day treatment centers, or hospital outpatient programs. If the student is severely emotionally disturbed, a sheltered workshop experience may be appropriate. Sheltered workshops allow the student to learn simple vocational tasks. If there is convenient access to a residential school, the student might attend the school portion of the program and return home daily.

Homebound Instruction

The most obvious reason for this, hopefully temporary, placement would be if an emotionally disturbed/behaviorally disordered student became bedridden because of a physical ailment. Homebound teachers visit students in their homes to give them the instruction they are missing in school. Because of the complexity involved in teaching *any* student, let alone one with emotional problems, high-quality homebound instruction can be difficult to secure.

It would be inappropriate to use this placement for students who exhibit severe behavioral problems in school, thereby making it serve as a type of school suspension. Rarely are homebound services equivalent to those offered in a full-day program. Students with emotional and/or behavioral problems are handicapped, that is, they do not behave in an unacceptable manner by choice. To deny them access to a viable school program is to deny them their right to an equal education because of their handicap.

Detention and/or Correction Facilities

This placement is usually not a school option. Among the residential placements it is clearly the least desirable as the judicial system is involved in the students' education. Some students with emotional and/or behavioral problems express their feelings in ways that get them into legal trouble. Thus, some researchers have reported that up to 40% of those labeled *juvenile delinquent* also have been found to be emotionally disturbed.

Students who are labeled delinquent may have committed acts that would not get them into trouble if they were adults. Such acts include truancy, inability to get along with parents, and use of alcohol or drugs. Many people believe that students should not be incarcerated, or adjudicated, if they exhibit such behaviors.

If children or adolescents commit crimes for which they would be arrested in the adult world, they would probably not avoid placement in a less restrictive setting.

Mental Health Clinics

This placement may supplement any of the previously listed services. Students may be referred to clinics as part of their school program or as an after-school activity. Professionals from clinics may also work with students during the school day.

Psychologists, psychiatrists, social workers, guidance counselors, and youth workers are some of the staff who may be affiliated with clinics with which a school may contract for services. They are rarely full-time employees of the school system, although many clinics have established long-term relationships with school districts.

Why refer my child to a clinic?

In some instances a child's problems can be best dealt with outside the public school. Sometimes clinics not only provide help from specialists who are not available in schools (e.g., clinical psychologists, social workers), but also opportunities for group counseling where students can meet and work with students having similar problems. Another benefit of clinics is that their services may be provided to students without having to take the students out of the regular school routine.

Residential Placements

A student may be placed in a residential setting for two reasons: lack of access to a viable community program and/or when the student's homelife contributes to his or her problems. Many communities do not have the resources necessary to help students with severe problems. In other instances, the homelife may contribute to the students' problems. However, removing them from their home setting should only happen as a last resort. Whenever possible, students must be taught to cope with their homelife. When the homelife is so destructive that removal is therapeutically necessary, it is important that students understand that removal from their home does not necessarily mean that it is *their* fault the family has problems. Most schools are reluctant to make such placements because they are very expensive.

Several types of residential placements, including foster homes and group homes, allow students to live in the same or a different community while attending a public school. In that school, they may be placed in a special education setting. Other types of residential placements include 24-hour care facilities that may be either medical (psychiatric or psychological) or educational in nature.

Does the placement of my child guarantee that his needs will be met?

Not necessarily. Before placement can be determined, a multidisciplinary team must identify the most appropriate program for a child. Identification of the students and selection of their placements are only two, albeit very important, concerns. The most important issue to consider is the type of program the student will receive in a given setting. A particular placement does not guarantee availability of a program that meets a specific student's needs.

For example, let's say that Joe needs to be placed in a setting that is very nurturing. He has a difficult time accepting orders from authority figures, including simple teacher demands such as, "Joe, please sit down. Class is starting." When given such instructions, Joe may shout at the teacher, screaming that he or she is not his parent, etc.

Yet, Joe is intelligent, almost to the point of being gifted, and if left alone, he can accomplish a considerable amount of work. His behavior, however, is such that he could not function well in a traditional regular class, and he needs help in the emotional/behavioral area. A special education teacher trained to work with Joe might help him deal with authority figures.

Consequently, a multidisciplinary evaluation team recommended a special education placement for Joe. Specifically, it was suggested that Joe be assigned to a special education classroom on a part-time basis, and attend those regular classrooms where his emotions/behavior would not interfere with his learning. While this is a logical recommendation, one very important ingredient is being overlooked—the philosophical makeup of this particular part-time special education setting.

Different approaches to treating students with emotional/behavioral problems exist. It is at this point in the placement process that these approaches take on particular significance. In the example of Joe, the part-time special education classroom may be very structured, with rules and consequences clearly stated and consistently followed. Further, the teacher may believe that students need to learn to follow rules in order to succeed in regular education classrooms. Most importantly, the teacher may believe that if she is inconsistent in following classroom rules, that is, bend them for some of her students, then the students will receive messages that rules are for only some students.

Enter Joe. His needs cannot be met with the philosophy of the classroom. Joe has difficulty taking directions and will openly rebel if they are given. The teacher, in order to demonstrate to her class that she is fair, feels that she must follow her behavioral orientation. Further, she believes that if she changes the classroom program for Joe, she will do major harm to the other 12 students in her room. If Joe is placed in this classroom, either he or the program is likely to suffer. This is a case where the use of a part-time special classroom seems to be appropriate, but the actual implementation will probably not work.

Other instances where this problem could occur are when students' learning styles dictate a specific approach and the classroom teacher does not use that approach. For example, in many resource rooms, teachers serve a variety of students who study different subjects at the same time. These teachers have to resort to such teaching and management techniques as worksheets, workbooks, and other types of seatwork for students who are not being directly taught at a given time. Yet, many of these students are placed in the setting because of their inability to sit still, complete seatwork, and so forth—students who need to have lessons explained or demonstrated to them in order to understand difficult concepts.

It is crucial that parents and professionals consider not only the label of children and their placements, but also the expectations of the teachers in those placements. Thus, it is the academic, social, and behavioral programming of the student, and not the placement, that should be adapted in order for the child to be successfully placed in the least restrictive environment.

Is it necessary for my child to live some place else?

As mentioned above, a student is usually referred to a residential treatment center as a last resort. Inadequate community treatment options are one reason for such placement, a problem that is not unusual in small communities. Remembering the least restrictive environment concept that was discussed above, the real issue behind having students live some place else is their inability to learn and live in their current placement/environment.

Some students may have problems that are so severe that continued living at home and public school attendance is simply out of the question. Also, and this is an equally sensitive issue, some family situations, either intentionally or unintentionally, may contribute to the students' problems in such a way that at least a temporary change is necessary. A placement away from the home can provide a "time-out" from a very difficult situation, allowing those involved to examine critical issues that may be causing problems and hopefully allow them to work on remediating those problems.

There is also the possibility that some students need more intensive help in either (or both of) the academic or emotional domains. While there are "trade-offs" to consider when making the decision of a residential placement, the notion of placing individuals in settings where they can learn to deal with their handicaps, and to not be handicapped by the setting itself, should be of primary importance.

Doesn't placement outside the home mean that I've failed as a parent?

Early in this book we mentioned that one of the least productive reactions to dealing with a child with emotional problems is blame. It is very easy to blame children (students) for their behaviors and emotions. It is also easy to blame ourselves for the way our children develop. Quite simply, what has happened, has happened. To examine and cross-examine the whys and wherefores only takes attention away from the main issue: how to resolve the problem at hand.

This is not to say that there may not be some shame (What will others think of *me* if Joe is sent to a residential school?) or guilt (Maybe this wouldn't have happened if . . .) associated with the decision to send a child to a residential school. If these feelings are very strong, the authors of this book recommend counseling. Many other families share the same feelings and problems. Sometimes support groups are available, or family counseling. Many residential schools, recognizing the need to include families in remediation, welcome family input and provide services to families.

What should my family say when asked about Tommy?

Your answer might vary depending upon the people to whom you are talking. You might decide to give more information to close friends. There is nothing shameful about somebody having problems. Thus, your response can be, "Tommy is going away to school to work on his problems."

An important message underlies your question. Tommy *has* problems that must be remediated. His problems may be due to a variety of things, most of which have been described in this book. Avoiding his problems may create more problems. Fabricating lies about Tommy's whereabouts might send mixed messages to Tommy. Are you ashamed of him? Is he a "freak" because he has these problems?

A common misconception about placing students in residential schools is that the process involves locking someone away in some medieval institution. Most residential facilities are very inviting and caring places, with more than adequate educational and living facilities. Upon the family's first visit to the school, it should be evident that Tommy isn't being sent away to some "crazy" house.

Finally, guilt and shame may only add to the problems Tommy is having. It is probably going to be a very difficult transition for Tommy without him also having to deal with your guilt and/or shame.

Summary

Many placement options are available to children and youth with emotional and behavioral problems. It is crucial to remember that gaining access to special education programs is only one hurdle to jump. Basic to *any* placement decision is that educational programs be designed to meet the individual needs of the students. It is from determining these needs that an appropriate placement can be chosen.

How Are Emotional and Behavioral Problems Treated?

6

 Treatment and intervention methods are of primary concern to persons who work with children and youth having emotional and behavioral problems, including parents, family members, and teachers. Current treatment methods are not based on a perfect science, as evidenced by children who fail to develop productive behavior in spite of professional intervention. Most individuals with emotional and behavioral problems can and do improve, however. Gains do not occur by accident and rarely do children outgrow their problems. Rather, behavioral and emotional improvements result from carefully formulated intervention programs and strategies. Several major treatment methods will be discussed in this chapter, including psychotherapy, behavior modification, and medication. Each of these procedures has been successfully used with children and adolescents and each offers unique advantages and disadvantages.

What is psychotherapy and how is it used with children and adolescents?

The term *psychotherapy* refers to any type of psychological or psychiatric treatment that is based on verbal or nonverbal communication. While different types of psychotherapy exist, they all rely on a discussion and/or interaction process; that is, they aim at improving behavior and mental health by means of having the person talk about personal issues and concerns. Thus, children are treated through discussions of their behavior, feelings, and motivations. Discussions may take place in individual sessions with a therapist or in groups of children having similar problems. With children for whom talking does not come easily or who are too young to discuss their problems, play is used to allow them to express their feelings, conflicts, and concerns. These intervention methods differ from drug treatment and other procedures which do not primarily rely on counseling, discussions of feelings, communication, and interaction programs.

What happens in psychotherapy?

It is difficult to say what actually occurs during psychotherapy since it may take many different forms. Most types of psychotherapy share several features, however.

First, psychotherapy relies on trust and a positive relationship between children and their therapist. Therefore, therapists can be expected to invest time in developing a positive atmosphere. For example, therapists may tell children that information shared during sessions will remain confidential, including being unavailable to parents and teachers. Therapists will also avoid being critical of a child, choosing instead to understand and accept the child's behavior and feelings. Such an atmosphere is needed for children to benefit from the therapy.

Second, psychotherapy relies on both children and therapists to be involved in the process. Children cannot sit back and expect the therapist to do all the work. Rather, both parties must try to understand the nature and basis of disordered behavior. Similarly, both children and therapists are involved in identifying appropriate solutions to problems.

Third, most psychotherapy programs focus on feelings and emotions. Children and adolescents will be encouraged to talk about how they *feel* about certain events and circumstances (e.g, their resentment at a parent's remarrying and the subsequent problem of having to share a bedroom with a new stepbrother).

Fourth, psychotherapy is based on self-understanding. Therefore, attention is focused on making children and adolescents aware of who they are and why they engage in certain behaviors, including responses considered to be maladaptive. Based on the underlying assumption that positive change can only occur with accurate self-understanding, children and adolescents are helped to understand their relationships with significant individuals in their lives, particularly parents.

Fifth, psychotherapy emphasizes an individual's unique perception of the world, that is, it recognizes that children and youth may interpret their world and the people with whom they interact in an individualized manner. Accordingly, therapists often attempt to understand and accept children's perceptions of their world—as opposed to directly changing such views—based on the belief that intervention must build on a child's or adolescent's unique feelings and perceptions.

Finally, much of what occurs in psychotherapy has its roots in psychoanalysis, although the latter may not constitute the treatment. Psychoanalysis will be discussed later.

One 3-year-old girl whose parents sought professional help because their daughter began to have sleeping and eating problems was assisted through play psychotherapy. In sessions with a professional therapist the child was able to reenact an experience with a relative who had stayed with her while her parents were out of town. Specifically, the child was able to express, without fear of betrayal or retribution, the anger and confusion she felt toward the relative who had sexually molested her.

Is there a difference between psychotherapy and psychoanalysis?

Yes, psychotherapy is a general term used to describe a number of verbally based therapeutic and counseling methods, including play therapy. *Psychoanalysis*, on the other hand, refers to a specific form of psychotherapy. Sigmund Freud, considered the founder of psychoanalysis, and his psychoanalytic method, developed in the 19th century, continue to have a significant influence on the manner in which children are educated and treated.

What is the history and theory of psychoanalysis?

Psychoanalysis is based on the notion that maladaptive behaviors are the result of underlying problems. *Underlying* is used here to describe conditions which cannot be seen (e.g., anger, resentment, personality conflict) but which cause overt problems. For example, parents may complain about a child's poor motivation in school, low grades, and inability to maintain friends. According to a psychoanalytic interpretation these *surface* behaviors (i.e., the overt problem behaviors of concern to parents and teachers) are caused by an underlying conflict or feeling of which the child may not be aware. Thus, psychoanalytic treatment does not focus on the immediate maladaptive behaviors (surface behaviors), adhering instead to the belief that significant and long-term improvement will come only as a result of understanding and removal of the underlying problem.

Psychoanalysis places great importance on children's early years, particularly their relationship with parents. Specifically, an early trusting relationship between parent and infant is crucial, and children's relationship with their mother is considered especially important in determining their future interpersonal dealings. Consequently, children who fail to establish trusting relationships with their parents may struggle with this issue throughout life. Additionally, unresolved conflicts or psychological crises during critical phases of development may set the stage for future problems.

Other significant characteristics of psychoanalysis include an emphasis on (a) unconscious motivation, (b) structure of personality, and (c) stages of personality development.

Psychoanalytic theory and thought are somewhat complicated, and an indepth discussion is beyond the scope of this book. Readers wishing more information on psychoanalysis are encouraged to obtain books on this topic from their public library.

What is "unconscious motivation" and how does it relate to emotional and behavioral problems?

A major assumption of psychoanalytic theory is that all of us (including children and adolescents) do things for reasons of which we are unaware. The origin of this part of psychoanalytic theory stems from Freud's belief that conscious motivation and awareness account for only a small portion of our behavior. Using the analogy of an iceberg, with the conscious awareness being the small part showing above the water and the unconscious the major portion of the iceberg below the surface, Freud believed that the unconscious largely determines our behavior. In psychoanalysis, therefore, the unconscious is most important for understanding and correcting emotional and behavioral problems. Psychoanalytic treatment programs, accordingly, involve attempts to make children and adolescents more aware of the reasons for their behavior.

What is meant by "structure of personality"?

According to psychoanalytic theory, personality is composed of three major parts: id, ego, and superego. Each part consists of unique characteristics, and all three interact to produce an individual's behavior and personality.

The *id* is the source of energy for the personality. This energy takes the form of *drives*, often of a sexual or survival nature. The id, the original system present at birth, operates on what is known as the *pleasure principle*—a basic desire to reduce pain and tension without concern for or knowledge about the objective and external reality. For example, in the case of a hungry child, the id is interested only in reducing hunger pangs without considering where the food comes from or how it is obtained.

The *ego* develops out of a need to deal with the objective world of reality. That is, the personality must have a rational way to respond to the id's demands and to interact with the everyday objective world. Operating on what is known as the *reality principle*, or logical and rational thinking, the ego mediates between the demands of the id and the reality of the world. Using the example of the hungry child again, the id demands that the hunger pangs be reduced and the ego subsequently searches for realistic ways to obtain food.

Finally, the *superego* is the part of one's personality which represents the moral standards of society, usually interpreted to us by parents and other adults. Thus, the superego becomes a judge of right and wrong for a child.

Together, the three aspects of human personality—id, ego, and superego—are thought to be the basis for our functioning and behavior. Emotional and behavioral problems may develop from any one of the personality components, because it is either poorly or overly developed. For example, children with inadequate ego development may have difficulty discriminating fantasy from reality; children with poorly developed superegos may be antisocial or delinquent; children with overly developed superegos, in turn, may exhibit guilt-ridden and rigid behavior.

What is meant by "stages of personality development"?

Freud believed that children pass through five stages of psychosexual development from infancy through adolescence: (a) the *oral stage*, birth to two years of age; (b) the *anal stage*, two to four years; (c) the *phallic stage*, four to six years; (d) the *latency stage*, age six until puberty; and (e) the *genital stage*, occurring at puberty.

During the *oral* stage the infant is largely stimulated and satisfied through activities that involve the lips and mouth. Eating, biting, and sucking are characteristic of behaviors observed during this period of development.

During the *anal* stage the child's attention shifts to the anus, whereby elimination of bodily wastes and toilet training take on primary importance.

At about the age of 3 or 4 the *phallic* stage sets in. Children's attention during this phase focuses on their sex organs. Also during this period, children are expected to resolve the so-called

Oedipus complex, the impulse to possess the opposite-sexed parent and take the place of the same-sexed parent.

The fourth stage, the *latency* stage, is often characterized by a relatively even balance between the id, ego, and superego functions. Thus, energy and attention are geared toward developing friends, learning in school, and engaging in social activities.

The happy balance in the latency phase is usually upset by the arrival of puberty and the *genital* stage, however. During this period adolescents must contend with a new wave of id impulses and experiences.

How do stages of personality development relate to emotional and behavioral problems?

According to psychoanalytic theory children may become fixated or arrested at certain stages of development. Such arrests occur for several reasons: When children are deprived at certain stages; when they are overly gratified at particular psychosexual periods; when children are resistant to moving to the next stage of development; or any one of a number of other physical or psychological events. Disturbed behavior is thought to result from an inability to resolve a conflict at a particular developmental stage or pass through a stage on schedule. For example, during the anal phase children's wish to move their bowels whenever they feel the urge usually conflicts with their parents' desire to toilet train them. Therefore, if toilet training is attempted too early or if it is too harsh or strict, children may rebel. Although these children ultimately develop appropriate toileting skills, psychoanalytic theory suggests that their anal-stage conflict may become an unconscious part of their personality and emerge later in characteristics such as disorderliness, resistance to rules, or extreme attention to neatness.

What happens during psychoanalysis?

Psychoanalysis with children and adults may be a lengthy process, sometimes lasting up to several years. Children may be seen by a therapist several times a week. In addition, their parents are typically also seen by a therapist at regular intervals in the course of their child's treatment. During the psychoanalytic process therapists attempt to help children gain insight, that is, recognize, understand, and accept their feelings and motivations, including unconscious urges and drives, and thereby gain improved emotional health and behavior. To achieve such insight and understanding children and youth examine past emotional experiences, some of which they may not be conscious of.

One 12-year-old boy received psychoanalytic treatment because of severe anxiety and fear of abandonment by his father and stepmother. In the course of several years of therapy the boy was helped to understand and accept his feelings associated with his biological mother leaving the family to live with another man. The mother left the family during a time when her son was attempting to resolve an Oedipal complex (phallic stage). That is, the boy was already experiencing natural feelings of competition with his father and an interest in assuming his father's relationship with his mother. Consequently, he came to believe that his feelings caused his mother to leave the family. Further, guilt over the situation led him to believe that his family would eventually banish him. Over several years of psychoanalysis the boy learned to understand his feelings, including his repression of the incident (pushing thoughts and feelings about the matter to an unconscious level).

Is psychoanalysis or psychotherapy used in education programs for emotionally and behaviorally troubled children?

Yes, the psychoeducational approach to educating children and adolescents with emotional and behavioral problems adapts psychoanalytic (and psychotherapeutic) principles for educational use. Accordingly, classroom personnel not only concentrate on teaching traditional academic content areas (e.g., reading, math), but attempt to understand the underlying motivation for their students' behavior. Additionally, since it is assumed that children's emotional well-being and their ability to learn in school are closely connected, attention is given to both students' feelings and their learning ability.

A teacher using a psychoeducational approach will concentrate on accepting students' feelings and attempt to bring such feelings to conscious awareness along with helping students understand how their feelings relate to their classroom behavior. For example, the teacher may tell a child, "You seem angry today—does it have anything to do with spending the weekend with your father"?

One specific psychoeducational approach is *life-space interviewing* whereby teachers or other adults help children deal with difficult situations or work through problems. Life-space interviewing involves children talking about *what* happened in a situation and finding alternatives so as to avoid the same problem in the future.

Educators using a psychoeducational approach view crises as opportunities for helping children and adolescents learn more productive behavior patterns. For example, one child who verbally provoked another youngster during recess was knocked to the ground. When the injured child complained to his teacher he was shown, through the teacher's use of a life-space interview, how his actions (taunting another student) resulted in his injury and how future occurrences might be avoided.

What is "behavior modification"?

Behavior modification, also known as the *behavioral model, applied behavior analysis, learning theory,* and *operant conditioning,* is used to describe a set of principles and procedures for understanding and systematically changing behavior. Most educational programs for behaviorally disordered and emotionally disturbed children and youth are based on behavioral procedures. Likewise, many therapists use behavioral procedures when working with children and adolescents.

How does behavior modification differ from psychotherapy and psychoanalysis?

Unlike traditional therapeutic approaches such as psychoanalysis, which consider maladaptive behavior symptoms of underlying psychological and emotional problems, behavior modification views problem behavior as targets for change. That is, behavior modification proponents do not support the notion that problem behaviors are signs of deep-seated emotional conflict, but rather consider them learned patterns of maladaptive behavior. According to this model, therefore, developing maladaptive behaviors is no different from learning adaptive responses. Thus, children may learn that they are able to manipulate their parents through tantrums or that hitting peers is an effective way to control others. Behavior modification principles are used to decrease maladaptive behaviors and increase adaptive responses which occur infrequently. In the preceding examples, tantrumming and hitting are viewed not as signs of unconscious or deep-seated problems, but as *the problems*, and procedures are subsequently developed to modify these behaviors.

What are some of the basic principles of behavior modification?

As mentioned, a basic rule of behavior modification is that maladaptive behaviors are learned and maintained in the same way as adaptive behavior. Accordingly, maladaptive behaviors of behaviorally and emotionally disturbed children and youth can be unlearned and replaced with more adaptive behaviors. Further, proponents of behavior modification do not accept the theory that problem behaviors are caused by unobservable psychological factors or that children's behavioral improvement must await progress in psychotherapy.

As a result of this fundamental principle, behavior modification deals with specific, observable behaviors. Behaviors identified for change, therefore, must be overt (e.g., taking out the trash, handing in math papers, hitting another child) and measurable. *Measurable* refers to behaviors that we can count or measure. Thus, instead of targeting hyperactivity for change (*hyperactivity* means different things to different people making it difficult to measure), the target for change might be *out-of-seat without permission* at school. Being out-of-seat without permission at school is a behavior that can be *seen, agreed upon,* and *counted.*

Another principle of behavior modification suggests that it is not necessary to assign a diagnostic label (e.g., emotional disturbance, schizophrenia) to children in order to treat them. Therefore, behavior modification practitioners attempt to improve behaviors that interfere with a child's adjustment without regard for how the child is diagnosed. For example, a child whose excessive pouting interferes with peer relationships would be exposed to procedures designed to reduce pouting and increase appropriate peer interactions. Whether or not the child had previously been identified as emotionally disturbed would not affect the manner in which the program is applied.

Behavior modification also maintains that the effectiveness of behavior change methods is not known until they have been tried. Thus, a procedure which has proven effective with one child cannot automatically be assumed to work equally well with another. Only by systematically applying and evaluating a behavior management procedure can its effectiveness be determined.

A final assumption of behavior modification is that most behaviors are controlled by events and experiences that happen before and after them. A child's tantrums, for example, might be the result of parental attention to crying and screaming. The significance of this principle for successfully modifying behavior is great: If we can isolate the events that support a behavior identified for change (e.g., attention-getting, manipulation of others), behavior problems may be replaced with more adaptive behavior.

Who uses behavior modification procedures with children and adolescents?

A variety of persons use behavior modification procedures, including therapists, teachers, and *parents*. Although successful use of these methods requires training and guidance one need not be a professional to do so. In fact, children often show the greatest gains when a variety of persons, including parents and family members, make consistent use of behavior modification.

What are the steps involved in using behavior modification with children and adolescents?

Four primary steps underlie successful behavior modification procedures: (a) identify, define, and measure the behavior to be increased or decreased; (b) determine where, when, and with whom the target behavior occurs; (c) identify events that may be promoting or maintaining the target behavior; and (d) apply intervention procedures. As noted earlier, these steps may be applied by a number of persons, including parents.

What's involved in identifying, defining, and measuring a behavior for change?

In accordance with the notion that problem behaviors are not symptoms of unconscious or underlying difficulties, behavior therapists attempt to modify (i.e., increase or decrease) the behaviors that interfere with a child or adolescent's adjustment. Thus, *specific, precisely defined behaviors* are identified for change. Examples include failure to follow parents' or teachers' commands, talking-out without permission at school, or kicking another person. All these behaviors may be measured, that is, a teacher, therapist, or parent can count the number of times they occur and can share with others their observations and interventions without interference of subjective interpretation and misunderstanding.

Why is it important to know where, when, and with whom a behavior targeted for change occurs?

As part of thoroughly understanding a target behavior, the person attempting to bring about a change must be familiar with the setting in which the behavior occurs and the circumstances surrounding it. For example, a child who displays negative behavior only in the presence of a babysitter would probably undergo a different intervention program than a child who displays such behavior around a number of people. Similarly, an adolescent who is considered a problem only during the dinner hour or in gym class at school would be dealt with differently than somebody who tends to have problems across different times and settings.

What is meant by "identifying events that may promote or maintain a problem behavior"?

As noted earlier, behavior modification is based on the assumption that we learn from experience to do particular things in particular ways. Thus, a toddler may learn that banging his head against a wall is an excellent way to gain his parents' attention (i.e., whenever he bangs his head someone attends to him) or that hitting effectively allows him to control a situation. Not all behaviors are so simply analyzed; however, identifying factors associated with the occurrence of a problem behavior is important. Accordingly, behavior modification involves attempts to uncover those factors which may be controlling a child's behavior and, subsequently, establish the most effective and efficient intervention program.

What are intervention procedures and how are they used with children and adolescents?

The responses of behaviorally disordered and emotionally disturbed children and youth can be changed by systematic use of consequences. *Consequences* refer to positive or negative events that happen *after* a child engages in a behavior that someone wants to increase or decrease. For example, a child may receive additional free time in the classroom *after* she successfully finishes her daily math assignments. Similarly, a student may lose his recess whenever he fights on the playground. Successful use of consequences requires that an agreed-upon intervention plan be followed each time a specified behavior occurs. Consequences can be of three types: (a) reinforcers, (b) planned ignoring (extinction), and (c) punishers (negative consequences).

What are reinforcers and how are they used with problem children and adolescents?

Reinforcers are consequences which increase the likelihood of future occurrences of a behavior. That is, children and youth are rewarded for specified behaviors in the hope that such positive consequences will increase the chances that the desired behavior reoccurs. For example, a teacher may verbally praise a child each time he holds up his hand to speak, or a youngster may be allowed to play a computer game at school if he completes an assignment within a specified time. In the preceding examples, teacher praise for seeking permission to talk and playing with a computer for successfully completing an assignment function as reinforcers if they increase the specified target behavior.

Reinforcers for children and adolescents usually fall into three categories: (a) social rewards (e.g., hugs and verbal praise for desired behavior); (b) tangible rewards (e.g., edibles and toys for displaying specified behavior); and (c) contingent activities (e.g., recess and free time for completing school assignments).

What is "planned ignoring" (extinction) and how is it used as a consequence?

Children and youth often seek attention by displaying unacceptable behavior. For example, a student may get out of his assigned school seat without permission to gain teacher attention or tantrum to control his parents' actions. *Planned ignoring* (extinction) involves systematic withdrawal of attention for unacceptable behavior followed by replacement of attention for desired behavior. Using this approach, a child may be ignored when she pouts but attended to when she engages in acceptable social behavior. Extinction may not work with every child. However, for children who are motivated by attention it may be an effective consequence.

How is punishment used to change the behavior of children and adolescents with behavioral and emotional problems?

Punishment means different things to different people. It may create an image of a trip to the woodshed for some and withdrawal of privileges for others. As part of behavior modification, *punishment* (or negative consequences) refers to any event which decreases a behavior it follows. For example, a child who reduces the number of fights he gets into as a result of losing bicycle privileges for fighting is said to have his behavior modified through negative consequences. Punishment programs for behaviorally disordered children and adolescents typically involve response cost, time-out, and overcorrection. Spanking and other forms of corporal punishment are rarely considered appropriate forms of behavior modification punishment.

What is "response cost" and how is it used as a negative consequence?

Response cost refers to systematic removal of rewards when specified unacceptable behaviors occur. For example, children may lose TV or other privileges for failing to abide by established rules and regulations.

How is time-out used with behaviorally and emotionally disordered children?

Time-out involves removing children from reinforcing situations whenever they display specified maladaptive behaviors. Time-out may require children and youth to sit quietly in a corner for short periods of time following unacceptable behaviors or otherwise restrict them from participating in reinforcing activities or being in reinforcing environments. One child was required to quietly lay his head on his desk for 3 minutes whenever he threw an object in class. Time-out is a popular intervention which has been used successfully by both professionals and parents.

What is "overcorrection" and how is it used with children and youth?

As a behavioral intervention procedure overcorrection consists of two main parts, *restitution* and *positive practice*. The first, restitution, requires that individuals who disturb or destroy things clean up or otherwise restore a situation to its original state. For example, an adolescent who purposefully throws food on the floor may be made to clean the soiled area. Positive practice, in turn, requires that a child or youth practice an appropriate behavior related to a maladaptive response. Thus, the adolescent who throws food may be required to transfer blocks from one container to another for several minutes. In this case, transferring blocks is an alternative behavior to throwing, which the youth is required to practice. Overcorrection is often a time-consuming and complex process; however, it offers an effective management procedure for children and youth with severe behavior problems.

What are the specifics of behavior modification programs for emotionally disturbed and behaviorally disordered children and youth?

Below are two sample behavior management programs for emotionally disturbed children. The first uses a reinforcement system, the second a punishment procedure.

Example 1

Positive Reinforcement

The subject was a 10-year-old boy in treatment at a psychiatric facility. He had been placed in the program as a result of extreme acting-out behavior. Although the child had made good progress, his teacher observed that he was slow and inconsistent in completing daily academic assignments, and that he had not responded well to attempts to motivate him to improve in this area.

As a result, the professional staff began to monitor the boy's completion of daily classroom assignments. Specifically, the target behavior was completion of daily spelling, history, and math papers on the day they were assigned and within the appropriate class period. Observations revealed that over a 5-day period the child completed about 20% of his assignments.

To increase the boy's schoolwork output a reinforcement program was used consisting of: (a) verbal praise following the submission of assignments; and (b) earning the privilege of being "staff man" on those days when at least 90% of his assignments were completed. As "staff man" the boy had an opportunity to aid the teacher in a variety of tasks in the school.

This reinforcement program greatly increased the child's work output. Specifically, within the first week of the program he was completing almost all his assignments. Because failure to hand in school assignments and follow adult directions were primary reasons for the child's original treatment referral, the intervention program was considered important to the youngster's overall well-being.

Example 2

Punishment Program: Response Cost

The subject of the program was a 4-year-old boy who was a residential patient in a state-operated psychiatric facility. The child was admitted to the program because his parents were unable to control his behavior.

As a part of his treatment plan, the child was assigned to a preschool classroom. School progress was slowed by his tendency to leave his seat without permission. The classroom teacher observed that whenever the youngster was not being attended to by an adult he would leave his seat and wander around the room. Several behavior modification programs, developed specifically to deal with this problem, had proven unsuccessful.

Finally, a response-cost punishment intervention was tried. The program consisted of notifying the child that the 5-point star he and his classmates received at the end of each school day would be altered if he did not stay in his seat. Specifically, he was told that he would be given a mark each time he got out of his seat without teacher permission. The marks were placed next to his name on the chalkboard. After he had received three marks, the teacher would take a pair of scissors and cut one of the points from his star. No loss of privileges were associated with the cutting of points from the star; however, staff did praise the boy when his star was complete.

This response-cost program successfully reduced the child's out-of-seat problem. Further, once he began staying in his seat his other behavior problems also subsided.

Are there forms of treatment which combine psychotherapy and behavior modification?

Yes, cognitive behavior therapy (CBT) is a combination of psychotherapy and behavior modification. Developed by psychologists, CBT is designed to integrate elements of the behavioral and traditional psychotherapeutic approaches.

In what way is cognitive behavior therapy a unique approach to helping children?

Based on the notion that people are disturbed because of their inaccurate perceptions of reality rather than arrested or delayed psychosexual development, CBT focuses on conscious, rather than unconscious thoughts, and the present rather than the past. As a result, teachers and therapists attempt to show children and adolescents that their perceptions are inaccurate, that is, they are not true. For example, some children may believe that others *shouldn't* tease them, or that teachers *must* be fair. While these expectations are desirable, reality is that other children do tease, and that some teachers may on occasion be "unfair."

CBT involves aiding children in identifying thoughts that upset them and analyzing why they are bothersome. Once these thoughts are understood, efforts are made to change them.

Will children who understand their thoughts be able to change their behavior?

In some cases, understanding how we think will encourage changes in behavior. However, for most people, understanding is not enough. For example, most people understand that weight gain is associated with eating certain types of food, such as ice cream and candy. Nevertheless, many people who are concerned about their weight do not change their diet. This is where the behavior modification approach is used in cognitive behavior therapy. Subsequent to thought-restructuring children and youth must practice their new patterns of thinking. Thus, many of the techniques described in the behavior modification section are used to encourage behavioral changes.

Professionals who use CBT work toward many of the same goals as do proponents of behavior modification. The major difference is that those who use CBT want children and youth to understand that their thinking patterns are often the cause of their problem behavior. Such understanding is thought to reduce similar problems in the future.

Are there different forms of cognitive behavior therapy?

CBT may be broken into several different types, including rational-emotive therapy, rational-behavioral therapy, rational-emotive education, reality therapy, and cognitive behavior modification.

Can medications cure children's and adolescent's behavioral problems?

As noted earlier in this book, there may be a relationship between physical and mental health and behavior. Thus, physicians are often included in diagnostic evaluations to rule out and/or treat physical bases for a disturbance (e.g., malnutrition, infections). Medications may be used to treat children and youth having emotional and behavioral problems; however, they do not cure behavioral and emotional problems.

What kinds of drugs are used with behaviorally disordered and emotionally disturbed children?

Prescription drugs, called *psychotropic medications*, are designed for certain problems and symptoms. Thus, specific drugs are used for hyperactivity (attention-deficit disorders) and problems related to mood, thought process, and behavior.

What kinds of medications are prescribed for hyperactive (attention-deficit disorder) children?

Central nervous system stimulant medications have become a popular intervention for children with short attention spans and hyperactivity. These drugs are thought to stimulate concentration and attention thereby reducing extraneous activity and behavioral problems. Although experts are unable to explain precisely how the drugs work, they do seem to have a positive effect on some children. Such medications typically produce beneficial results only for prepuberty children and, thus, are usually not used with adolescents.

Common central nervous system stimulants include Benzedrine, Ritalin, Cylert, and Dexedrine. Side-effects of these medications tend to be minimal, although there have been reports of appetite loss and insomnia.

Central nervous system stimulant drugs do not work with all children. Thus, well-formulated evaluation programs must be designed for children receiving these treatments.

What kinds of drugs are used to treat aggressive and acting-out children and adolescents?

Severe problems, including emotional outbursts and bizarre, self-stimulatory, stereotypic, and aggressive behavior, are often treated with powerful drugs known as *major tranquilizers* or *phenothiazines*. Specific forms of these medications include Thorazine, Mellaril, Trilafon, Stelazine, and Prolixin. A *butyrophenones* drug, Haldol, has also been used with some success. Although they may reduce disorganized thinking and hallucinations of children and youth with psychotic conditions (e.g., schizophrenia) and generally help in managing individuals with severe behavioral problems, these drugs are often associated with severe side-effects. In particular, marked drowsiness, blurred vision, impaired motor performance, anemia, and signs of Parkinsonism sometimes occur.

Less extreme emotional problems may be treated with *sedative* or *antianxiety* drugs. These medications, including Atarax, Vistaril, and Equanil, are sometimes used to reduce anxiety and hyperactivity and to induce sleep. Similar drugs, including Valium, Librium, Clonopin, and Tranxene have anticonvulsant properties and, thus, may be prescribed for children who have seizure disorders. Sedative and antianxiety drugs tend to have fewer side-effects than major tranquilizers.

Are there drugs for treating depressed children and adolescents?

Antidepressant drugs, as suggested by the name, are used to treat depression. Children with symptoms of depression have been treated with *tricyclic antidepressants*, the most common of which is Tofranil. Another category of antidepressant drugs, *monoamine oxidase inhibitors*, commonly abbreviated as MAO, have primarily been used with adults. The effectiveness of antidepressant drugs with children has yet to be clearly established; thus, use of these medications should be considered experimental.

What is the role of drug intervention methods with emotionally and behaviorally disordered children and youth?

Medications can have profound impact on health and behavior. Accordingly, drug treatment must be considered a viable option for helping problem children and youth. However, drugs are not a cure for social and emotional problems; therefore, they must be used only to support other treatments such as behavior modification and psychotherapy. Additionally, drugs are not appropriate or effective with all children. Consequently, systematic evaluation and monitoring must constitute an important part of any drug-treatment effort. For every child or adolescent treated with psychotropic medications, medical personnel, educators, mental health workers, and families must work closely together to determine the drug's benefit.

Summary

In this chapter we have identified and discussed major ways to deal with the emotional and behavioral problems of children and youth. In spite of the value of each, no single approach is complete or adequate with every child. The best treatment results occur when a combination of procedures is used. Thus, children and adolescents who are helped by cross-sections of professionals (e.g., educators, mental health workers, medical personnel) using a variety of treatment approaches (e.g., psychotherapy, behavior modification) based on the children's needs make the best progress. Additionally, for optimal progress to occur, parents and families must play an integral part in the overall treatment and education process.

What Can Parents and Families Do to Help?

Many of today's technological and scientific advances give the impression that we control our world. Space exploration, test-tube babies, heart transplants, computerized homes, and similar achievements suggest that we have the ability to manipulate the world with the flip of a switch. Yet, we need go no further than the daily newspaper to be reminded of how vulnerable we are. Problems abound! Many of these are of an interpersonal nature and seemingly lack satisfactory solutions. Thus, it is surprising that scientists can launch space shuttles, but are unable to stop adolescent suicide and academic failure. In an age of almost limitless potential, we continue to live with a number of the same problems that faced our ancestors. Yet, research and practice have produced some effective ways to aid persons with emotional and behavioral problems. Some of these measures, particularly those appropriate for use by parents and families, are discussed in this chapter.

How important is parent and family involvement?

There is no question that children are influenced by their parents and families. In fact, no other single experience impacts so profoundly on the way we react to the world and its people. Our values, attitudes, and unique ways of behaving are often a direct result of parent and family influence. This is not to suggest that children and adolescents will not develop behaviors that are uniquely their own; that they will not rebel against or reject certain family traditions and values; or that they will not be influenced by others, such as peers. Additionally, as discussed in an earlier section, parents are not always the cause of their children's problems. Science has yet to determine why children and youth develop emotional and behavioral problems. In some instances, parents' personal problems and poor child-rearing practices may be to blame. In other instances, however, parents do not appear to be the cause. Yet, regardless of whether parents and families are responsible for their children's problems, they can help find solutions. In fact, parent and family support is necessary for children's optimal growth and development. In this regard, the role of parents and families may include acting as (a) referral agents; (b) support agents; and (c) advocates for their children.

What do I do as a referral agent?

Parents often find that the professionals they respect the most and have most contact with do not share their concern over their children's behavior. In response to a parent's concern about her child's behavior, pediatricians or family physicians, for example, may suggest that the child is going through a phase or that a given concern is unfounded. One mother observed that every time she attempted to talk to her family doctor about her son's problems, the doctor wanted to write a prescription for tranquilizers. In spite of exceptions to this pattern, many parents find it difficult to find suitable professional help for their children.

Parents can take a number of steps to insure that pediatricians and other physicians note their concerns. First, make it clear that you are not asking your doctor to personally solve the problem. Explain that you are concerned about your child's behavior and are seeking an assessment by a professional trained and experienced to work with children and adolescents with emotional and behavioral problems. Physicians often lack the time and expertise to deal with emotional problems. Thus, emphasize that you are not asking your doctor to solve the problem on the spot.

Second, document your concerns. Rather than telling your pediatrician, "My child doesn't get along with other children.", attempt to identify precisely what it is your child is doing. For instance, does *not getting along* mean that he prefers to play by himself?; that he fights with other children?; or that he is the neighborhood bully? Further, report how often and how intensively the problem occurs, and for what length of time. Specifying that your child tantrums violently 3–4 times per day for 1–2 hours and that this behavior has occurred consistently over the past year is far more meaningful than simply relating that your child tantrums. Child development records and other documents which show patterns of emotional growth and development may also be useful in voicing your concerns.

What should I do if my doctor doesn't share my concern?

Seek help for your child's behavior even if your doctor does not share your concern. If you have observed unusual behavior patterns over extended periods of time (e.g., extreme withdrawal for 3–6 months or more), seek outside professional help. Your child's problem may turn out to be insignificant and temporary. However, if you consider it significant and if it is disruptive or bothersome to you and your family, contact the appropriate professional. The best source of referral information is your community or county mental health agency.

Can referrals for service be made by and through school personnel?

Yes. In fact, most children with emotional and behavioral problems are identified during their school years. As a result of classroom and school requirements, children who fail to abide by established rules and regulations and who have difficulty getting along with others are usually identified by teachers and other educational personnel and, in many instances, parents are first told of a behavioral or emotional concern by their child's teacher. Thus, classroom teachers are effective evaluators of children's behavior and discussions with teachers regarding your child's behavior should be valuable sources of information.

As in dealings with medical personnel, teacher contacts are most productive when concerns are specific and documented. That is, tell your child's teacher exactly what your concern is; how frequently and intensively the problem occurs; and how long it has been going on. Public schools are required to provide assessment and educational services for handicapped children and youth, including those with serious behavioral and emotional problems. Thus, you may secure an evaluation for your child at no cost to you. If it is agreed that your child has a problem that should be investigated, ask the teacher to initiate a referral for evaluation.

What if the teacher doesn't think my child has a problem?

If a teacher does not agree that a problem exists, you may still request an evaluation. Such a request should be made if you and your family have reason to believe your child has a serious problem. To request an evaluation, *write* the director of special education in your local school district. If you don't have the individual's name and address, call the board of education or school administration office in your city. Your letter should specify the basis for your concern; request a district evaluation; and be accompanied by copies of relevant background documents (e.g., evaluation reports, developmental charts). School districts are required by state and federal mandate to consider parental requests for evaluation.

What does it mean to be a "support agent"?

Children with emotional and behavioral problems seldom make significant improvement unless the meaningful individuals in their lives work together. Thus, parents cannot expect their child to be "cured" exclusively by therapy, professional counseling, or special education. Rather, parents and professionals must work together. Parents' role in this regard will vary, but it can be expected to include cooperation and support for agreed-upon plans. In many instances, counselors, teachers, and mental health professionals develop plans for parents and families to follow. Parents may be asked, for example, to establish and maintain certain rules; take certain actions; or collect and/or provide certain types of information. For children to benefit the most, parents must support agreed-upon decisions and recommendations. Not only should parents and families be involved in decision making, once a decision has been reached, they must also support it.

What does being an "advocate" mean?

The dictionary defines *advocate* as "one who represents or acts in support of another." In the case of parents of emotionally disturbed or behaviorally disordered children, advocacy means that children's interests receive priority status. Although this may lead parents to view their situation differently from professionals, it does not mean that parents should disagree with, distrust, or otherwise resist cooperating with professionals. Conversely, parents should not unthinkingly accept all recommendations and suggestions without considering child and family needs as well as alternative recommendations. Parents and professionals must strive for a partnership in which both parties have the right to voice their opinions and to disagree. Such an open relationship strengthens the partnership and ultimately improves services to children.

The parents of a 16-year-old autistic-like boy found themselves caught between loyalty to their local school district and their son's interests. The school district had historically been responsive to their child's needs, including starting an elementary program for autistic-like and severely emotionally disturbed children. When the boy outgrew the elementary program, however, the district did not have available a suitable alternative. Instead, school personnel recommended that the boy be placed in a high-school learning disability program since that was the only service available. The parents found themselves in the uncomfortable position of wanting to support the school district, but knowing that the recommended service was not in their son's best interest. Open discussion of concerns between school staff and parents led the district to contract for appropriate services from a neighboring district. Only by advocating for their son—putting their child's interests first—were these parents able to secure a suitable program.

Can parents be effective advocates for their children and still cooperate with professionals?

Parents of behaviorally and emotionally disturbed children must seek to cooperate with professionals. However, cooperation does not mean passive compliance with suggestions and strategies which may not be in a child's best interests. Thus, parents must trust and support the professionals with whom they interact while keeping their child's interests a priority.

How important are rules for children and adolescents?

Parents of behaviorally and emotionally disturbed children and youth often experience difficulty with rule enforcement and behavior management. Since success in this area is often basic to children's improvement and family tranquility, it merits serious attention.

What can I do to set good rules?

Children and adolescents may claim they do not need rules. Yet, the structure that comes from knowing limits and expectations is both necessary and beneficial. Setting and implementing rules involves several steps.

1. *Rules should be purposeful.* For instance, a rule may state that a child will not play in the street *because it is dangerous*; or that loud music will not be played in the house after 7:00pm on school nights *because it would interfere with doing homework*. Thus, each rule should be designed to accomplish a specific goal, usually to protect a child or to maintain order. Such clarity requires that both a *specific* target behavior (e.g., failing to take the trash out, as opposed to "not minding") and a *specific* conse-quence (loss of bicycle privileges for 24 hours, as opposed to "something you will regret") be identified. Rules should also specify rewards for compliance as opposed to negative conse-quences for noncompliance. Rules should not be designed simply to demonstrate control. Telling a child he cannot do certain things merely to show that you are in charge and can control his behav-ior is unacceptable. Additionally, children must not be expected to do things they cannot understand or perform. For example, it is unrealistic to expect an academically deficient high-school student to make straight As (as opposed to *improving* his grades) or a nonverbal autistic child to talk before he is allowed to eat.

2. *Attempt to involve children.* Children tend to be more accepting of rules they have helped develop. Such involvement will vary with children's age and ability. Yet, almost all children can be involved to some extent. In some cases, parents may simply explain why a rule is being implemented (e.g., "You cannot play in the street because you might get hurt."). Other situations require more discussion. Thus, the parents of a teenager who has consistently abused her car privileges might enter into discus-sions regarding the use of the family car (e.g., "Terri, your mother and I are concerned over your abuse of car privileges—I want us to talk about some rules for your use of the car."). Given the opportunity for involvement children and adolescents will be more likely to accept and abide by rules.

3. *Limit the number of rules.* "The fewer the better" is a good rule on rules. Children and adults not only have difficulty remembering long lists of rules, they tend to consider them meaningless and take them less seriously.

4. Establish fair and appropriate consequences. Particularly with children who have behavior and emotional problems, it is important to pay attention to rule compliance and noncompliance. First, children must understand precisely what will happen if they comply or fail to comply with rules (e.g., "If you study from 7:00–8:30pm Monday through Thursday, you may use the car Friday and Saturday night."; "If you hit your sister you must sit quietly in the corner for 3 minutes."). Only when such understanding is assured can consequences be applied. Additionally, parents must make sure that consequences are reasonable and enforceable. Consequences must not be too light or too severe. Similarly, impulsive and unenforceable consequences must be avoided (e.g., "You are grounded for a year."; "You'll never, ever use the car again."). Also, parents must be able to enforce established rules. For example, avoid telling an adolescent that he cannot use *his* car unless he follows specified rules when you have no means of enforcing such a rule.

5. Be consistent. A consequence must occur *every* time a rule condition is not met. This requires that adults are willing to apply the consequence any time the target behavior occurs, even if it happens at a highly inopportune time. Additionally, in applying consequences parents should attempt to adhere to the following guidelines: (a) do not argue and negotiate—when a rule infraction occurs, apply the stated consequence with a minimum of explanation and without allowing an argument to develop; (b) avoid emotional displays when applying the consequence—do what you said you would do in a straightforward, business-like manner. Demonstrating to children that you are hurt or upset usually has little positive effect; (c) apply the consequence after rule conditions have been met—never before. Telling a child, for example, that you have decided to provide him an agreed-upon trip prior to his meeting the conditions for the trip often has a negative effect on the overall behavior management program.

6. *Use positive as well as negative consequences.* It is not unusual for parents (and children!) to think of rules exclusively in negative terms. Thus, for example, families may think only in terms of what a child will lose if he or she violates a rule. Rules tend to work best when rewards (including praise and attention) accompany negative consequences.

Are there other things I can do to manage my child's behavior?

Yes. One option is to *follow routine schedules.* Children and adolescents tend to be positively influenced by structure and routines. For example, having set bedtimes, study times, and meal times often aids children in understanding and following schedules and parental requests. Problems may occur when children are unable to anticipate events and activities. This does not mean that parents and families must never vary their schedules—such a practice is neither realistic nor desirable. However, basic schedules and routines have been found to reduce management problems.

Another management idea is to *plan activities for children.* This does not mean that something must be scheduled for every waking minute—this would not only be burdensome for parents but a problem for children. However, behavioral problems are most apt to occur during unstructured times. Thus, parents may discuss with their offspring which activities are available to them after school and on weekends (e.g., model building, ball playing, bicycling, summer camp). Although an activities list often does not appeal to children (e.g., "I don't want to do that!"), parents will probably discover that the more involved children become in structured and productive activities, the less likely they are to engage in deviant acts.

An additional management reminder is to refrain from nagging and lecturing to your child. Instead, establish and follow through on appropriate responsibilities, expectations, and rules.

Are there management programs designed to increase or decrease specific behaviors?

Rules and other general management techniques may fail to change some behaviors. In such situations more structured management techniques may be necessary. Such methods are best applied under professional direction. Although parents are usually able to successfully use behavior change methods, these stricter procedures should be set up and followed by a trained professional.

What are the steps in a behavior management program?

Several steps are involved in setting up and carrying out an effective behavior management program:

Step 1: Identify a specific behavior to be increased or decreased. Behavior management programs work best when applied to well-defined behaviors. For example, attempting to change a behavior such as "hyperactivity" or "bad attitude" is difficult because the target behavior may differ in the eyes of various people, including the child. One parent might define "bad attitude" as failing to follow parental directions while another may view it as kicking family members. As a result, parents wishing to change a behavior must specifically define it.

What is involved in "specifically defining a behavior"?

Definitions should include the following: *what* the behavior is; *where* the behavior will be observed and dealt with; and *when* the behavior will be observed and dealt with. The *what* requires that parents precisely define a behavior. For example, *hitting* might be defined as a child making contact with another person with his fist, hand, or arm. In this definition no attempt is made to differentiate between soft and hard hits, or purposeful or accidental hitting. A hit is a hit! The *where* identifies settings, specifically those sites where the target behavior will be observed and dealt with. For example, a program for hitting might be applied at home or at the babysitter's, but not at the store, particularly if it is impossible to carry out the consequence in a store setting. The *when* part of the definition specifies the times during which the program will be applied (e.g., 7:00–8:30pm Monday–Friday). When considering the above three elements, parents have a much greater chance of successfully changing a behavior.

Are there other definition issues I should consider when attempting to change my child's behavior?

Yes. It is important to make sure that the behavior you wish to change is under the child's control; otherwise, it cannot be changed through this management system. Slamming a door, saying "thank you", and throwing rocks at the family cat are under a child's control. In contrast, sweating and tics are examples of behaviors generally not under an individual's control, and thus not usually subject to change using these techniques.

What are the other steps in setting up a behavior management program?

Step 2: Determine the settings and situations surrounding the problem. This simply means that you should examine the conditions associated with the problem. Does the behavior only occur around certain people (e.g., mother, babysitter) or at certain times (e.g., dinner, bedtime)? Identifying these factors is helpful. For example, if it can be determined that a child has a certain problem only with his father, the solution may involve improving their relationship rather than developing a formal management program.

Step 3: Evaluate what you do when the behavior occurs and what you have done in the past to change the behavior. In dealing with their children's behavior parents and families resort to a number of methods, some of which are more successful than others. For example, children may be talked to, spanked, made to feel guilty, given an allowance for following rules, and so forth. Knowing what option has worked in the past is a basic step in planning for the future. In addition, attempt to understand your own and other family members' reactions to a given problem. For instance, one mother, who was extremely concerned about her daughter's reluctance to play with other children, realized that her response to this problem might be maintaining it. Thus, she observed that when her child came home from school she immediately began nagging her to go outside and play with neighborhood children. Apparently the child enjoyed her mother's attention, even though it was negative, because when the mother ceased nagging, the child began playing with other children. After the child played with her peers her mother talked to her and gave her attention, a procedure which further increased her playing with peers.

Step 4: Select and apply suitable consequences. After defining a behavior and the circumstances surrounding it, apply appropriate methods for changing it. Four major types of consequences may be considered: positive consequences, ignoring, negative consequences, and environmental changes.

Step 5: Evaluate the effectiveness of your management methods. The effectiveness of behavior management consequences and methods will vary with specific children and conditions. Thus, a technique may work with some children and not with others. Therefore, it is essential to evaluate a program. Without such evaluation parents may continue to use ineffective methods or drop an effective procedure.

What are "positive consequences" and how are they used?

Positive consequences are events which increase a behavior. Two major forms of positive consequence are *contingent activities* and *social consequences*. Contingent activities, also known as "Grandma's law," make preferred activities dependent upon desired behavior. For example, children or adolescents may be told, "When you finish your homework you may watch TV."; "You may ride your bicycle after you take out the trash."; or "If you avoid hitting your brothers and sisters this afternoon, you may stay up an extra 30 minutes." As illustrated, a desired activity is used to encourage a specific, desirable behavior.

Social consequences include praise, parental attention, smiles, and hugs for desired behavior. When used consistently, these forms of human contact and appreciation are powerful motivators. Thus, parents may recognize their children for specific deeds (e.g., "I apppreciate your good manners."), realizing that when such attention consistently follows desired behavior the behavior will be repeated.

How is ignoring used as a behavior management technique?

Ignoring may decrease problem behaviors which occur as a result of attention. For instance, a child who tantrums to make her parents give in to her demands may cease this behavior if family members ignore her when she begins to cry.

When attempting to change a behavior through ignoring consider the following: (a) at first ignoring may increase a behavior. That is, children may initially try to gain attention by increasing the problem behavior; (b) ignoring works only if everyone involved is able to ignore. In instances where children are ignored only some of the time and by some people, the system will fail.

It is also extremely important to keep in mind that in order to decrease a behavior through ignoring you must give attention for acceptable behavior. Thus, you must ignore behavior you want to decrease while paying attention to behavior you want to increase. If you fail to give attention for suitable behavior you won't be able to decrease a negative behavior through ignoring.

What are negative consequences and how are they used?

Negative consequences or punishment (see Chapter 6 for additional discussion) refer to undesirable events which follow specific behaviors. For example, children may learn they will lose privileges (e.g., leaving the yard, riding their bicycle, going to the show) if they do certain things.

What kinds of negative consequences are available for use by parents and families?

A number of different negative consequences are available, one of which is *time-out*. Time-out involves placing a child in a chair in a corner (or similar spot) when he or she displays a certain unacceptable behavior. For example, a child may be required to sit quietly for 3 minutes in a chair in the corner of the living room if he throws things in the house. When used correctly, this popular consequence has led to positive results. Time-out is most effective if used with specific behaviors. Timing kids out for a variety of unacceptable behaviors usually reduces the effectiveness of this management tool. Additionally, the time-out site should be clear of toys, TV, and other interesting things, including people. Thus, parents and family members must ignore children in time-out. Further, time-out sessions should be short. Three to 5 minutes of quiet have proven best. If children are crying at the end of the specified time, time-out should be extended until the crying stops. Finally, the circumstances surrounding the unacceptable behavior should not be discussed until after the time-out period. Thus, parents or others using time-out should limit their comments to the child (e.g., "No kicking; go to time out.") until the time-out period is over.

What does "changing the environment" mean and how is it used as a management method?

Changing the environment may take a variety of forms, including any change in conditions which may be causing problems. For example, one child threw severe tantrums whenever forced to eat hominy. Since this was the only food that provoked this behavior and because hominy was not considered essential to the child's survival, the problem was dealt with by eliminating hominy from her diet. Another parent solved her toddler's habit of throwing objects from the top of coffee tables and other furniture by moving the material out of the child's reach. In yet another situation it was determined that the child was most apt to be destructive when she did not have something to do. As a result, her parents developed a list of activities she could do. As suggested by these examples, simple methods are often sufficient for dealing with problems.

What does evaluation involve?

Evaluation ordinarily requires daily monitoring of the target behavior. Parents are advised to seek the help of a psychologist or other qualified mental health worker or educator when developing evaluation methods.

Are there things parents can do to make sure programs work?

Behavior management programs will not work 100% of the time. However, the best results occur when the following basic steps are followed: First, apply a consequence only *after* a target behavior. Do not allow a child to engage in a desired activity because you have faith he will complete an agreed-upon chore, for example. Rather, wait till he completes the chore. Similarly, do not place a child in time-out because she *looked* like she was going to engage in some undesirable activity. Second, apply the consequence consistently. Carry out whatever you said you would do each time the behavior occurs. Third, apply the consequence as soon after the target behavior occurs as possible. Waiting diminishes the strength of the consequence. Fourth, make a commitment to apply a procedure over time. Behavior management programs sometimes work quickly—on other occasions they take time. However, unless they are used consistently for significant periods of time they will probably not be successful. Thus, don't stop using a program when it starts to work. It is sometimes tempting to drop a procedure when the target behavior improves, but most programs stop being effective when parents stop working to apply them! Fifth, seek professional guidance when setting up a behavior management program. Once a program has been decided upon, it is important that you follow the plan and not make changes in what was agreed upon.

Is there more to dealing with a problem child than using rules and management techniques?

Dealing satisfactorily with a child or adolescent who has emotional and behavioral problems requires more than sound rules and management techniques. Parents and family members must listen and communicate with their offspring.

What does it mean to "listen" to my child?

Listening, especially *effective listening,* is not as easy as one might think. Children and adolescents have often observed that their parents do not listen to what they have to say. For example, the following comments are typical.

"I get a lecture every time I try to talk about a problem I have."

"My parents get angry and yell at me whenever I try to honestly tell them how I feel."

"My mother never has time to listen to me. Whenever I try to talk to her she tells me, 'Hold that thought—I'll get back to you'."

"Every time I try to talk to my parents they end up giving me their opinion or what they consider to be *the answer*. They never let me talk it through with them."

"My dad never really listens to me. After a few minutes he interrupts me and says every kid has the same thoughts and feelings. He just tells me to 'hang in there' and everything will be all right."

On the other side of the communication barrier, parents have observed that their children fail to listen to them. Some typical parent observations are noted below.

"My kid never tells me anything—At the dinner table I ask him what he did at school and he says 'nothing'."

"At the end of a busy day I have little patience to listen to my kid. Every kid has problems, but she'll work them out, just like everyone else."

"My son resists my becoming a part of his life. Whenever I take an interest in what he's doing or ask questions about school he tells me to mind my own business."

"I try to give my daughter some advice. Yet, every time I try to tell her something she tells me things have changed since I was in school."

"My daughter will ask me for my advice and then do just the opposite of what I suggest. I don't know what good it does to discuss things with her."

"Every time I try to talk to my daughter about something important she says, 'Oh mother!' and walks away."

The above comments all reveal a desire to communicate—people have a strong need to be heard and understood. Yet, children and their parents are not always able to satisfy this need, particularly when children and youth with problems are involved.

How do I go about communicating with my child?

Children and adults must feel accepted and valued. People often go to great lengths to satisfy this need, including acting in ways which appear the opposite of how they feel. For example, a child may tell his parents that he doesn't want to be a part of the family or that he doesn't care whether they are interested in his well-being. Thus, children may say the opposite of what they feel as a way of protecting themselves from rejection (e.g., "You don't care about me—Just leave me alone, I don't need you."). In spite of what they may say, children and adolescents will strive to satisfy and protect their need for acceptance and love, both at home and away from home.

What can I do to help my child feel loved and valued?

Parents can help their child meet this basic human need by adhering to the following recommendations.

Set aside time to talk to your child. Developing a relationship which fosters communication takes time and effort. Thus, parents must not expect that their children will *talk* with them only during problem periods or when parents consider it necessary. Good relationships must develop! To increase the likelihood of parents and children talking arrange times for such discussions—perhaps before or after dinner or whenever both parties have at least 30 minutes available. Parents should not push their children to talk about their problems. Rather, they should concentrate on spending quality time with their children, perhaps while engaging in games and other informal activities. The trust developed through such activities often increases children's willingness to discuss issues with their parents.

Listen without lecturing or making suggestions. Adults often forget that the problems their children deal with are the same they dealt with only a few years earlier. It is very easy, for example, for parents to observe that childhood friendships will endure the crisis of wearing the same color dress to the prom; or that being rejected by a friend is not the biggest problem one will encounter. Similarly, it is tempting for parents to tell their children how they should feel; what they should do; or that their problems are relatively insignificant. Thus, parents should try to understand children's feelings and problems rather than giving advice or suggestions. When children want advice and are ready to accept it, they will ask!

Use eye contact, a basic feature of good listening. Poets and writers have reminded us that the eyes are pathways to understanding. In a less formal manner, children have made the same observations (e.g., "My dad says he's listening to me while he's reading the paper—I can't believe he's listening, though, when he hides behind the paper."). The message is simple: Listening requires the use of both the ears and the eyes.

Be aware of emotion. Messages are generally of two types. The first consists of the actual content of a conversation, the *overt theme* (e.g., "Can I spend the night with Kathy?"; "What's for dinner?"). The second relates to the emotion which accompanies an overt message. Tone, gesture, and expression are cues to emotion. Being sensitive to these feelings often helps parents focus their remarks. For example, a child who enters the house and angrily observes, "School is such a waste of time and teachers are so stupid," is expressing his feelings and probably a need to talk. Under such conditions parents are likely to find their child to be more responsive and subsequent discussions to be more productive when they use comments such as, "Sounds like you had a rough day at school.", instead of lecturing about the need to respect authority; the benefits of a formal education; or accusatory remarks (e.g., "Now what did you do"?).

Be aware of problem "ownership". Many parents find it difficult to accept that they are not responsible for all their offspring's problems. As children become older and more independent they assume adult rights and responsibilities. Even if inclined to do so, parents cannot assume responsibility for all their children's problems. Parents must be able to listen to their children, support them, and aid them in making decisions. At the same time, they must allow their children to assume responsibility for their own problems. This does not mean that parents should be unconcerned or disinterested, however.

The parents of a 15-year-old boy were distressed over their son's poor grades and lack of academic motivation. Both parents were college graduates and expected their son to follow in their path. The boy, however, was uninterested in school. Grades were a constant source of friction, with the parents taking personal responsibility for their son's failures. Consequently, they often discussed between themselves and with their friends their shortcomings, noting that if they had taken the correct actions or done the right things their son would not be experiencing school problems. Not until they were counseled to allow their son to deal with *his* problem (rather than their problem) did the situation improve. The parents maintained an interest in their son's school progress, established study hours, and reinforced school achievement. However, they learned to allow their son to assume responsibility.

Be a "real" person in the presence of your child. Few parental responsibilities are formally taught. Thus, parents make mistakes and engage, at times, in less-than-perfect child-rearing practices. One such tendency is to assume a stoic posture and attitude, believing that children must be exposed to unfeeling and unceasingly moralistic parents. One teenage girl described her need to discuss "boys and sex", but noted that she was unable to do so with her mother. This reluctance stemmed from the impression that her mother did not show much interest in the topic and that "Mom and I have never been able to talk about such things." Yet, other women often sought out her mother as a confidante, particularly on interpersonal and sexual issues. This parent was able to discuss sensitive matters with others, but not with her daughter. Although it is not always easy, parents should show the same sensitivity and willingness to discuss matters with their children as they do with others.

How can I improve my communication skills?

Most of us have friends with whom we feel comfortable talking and with whom we are able to share both information and feelings. These individuals create an atmosphere of give-and-take, trust, and mutual respect.

For a variety of reasons few parents are able to establish this type of relationship with their children. Instead, frustration, limited understanding, and minimal acceptance are more common. Yet, communication can be improved.

The following discussion between an 11-year-old and his mother is typical of many parent-child interactions:

Child: "I'm not doing so hot in school this year. The teacher doesn't like me—she's always yelling—and my grades . . . Boy, my grades."

Parent: "What have you been doing? You'd better start studying or your father will be furious!"

Put yourself in the child's place. Regardless of the parent's intentions this boy will most likely (a) walk away angry, embarrassed or hurt; (b) feel compelled to argue with his mother; or (c) vow never again to share information and feelings. The interaction suffers from poor communication and a lack of understanding of feelings and circumstances.

Alternatives for dealing with the situation exist. Consider, for example, the following:

Child: "I'm not doing so hot in school this year. The teacher doesn't like me—she's always yelling—and my grades . . . Boy, my grades."

Parent: "Things are not exactly going the way you wanted, are they?"

Child: "Yea . . . I really wanted to do better this year . . . to make things different . . . I don't know what's going to happen."

Parent: "Your intentions were good—but things are not working out."

Child: "Maybe you and Dad can help me with math. I still don't think that teacher is ever going to like me, no matter what I do."

Parent: "Sounds like you may have some ideas for improving things."

In the above example the parent used several basic effective communication procedures:

1. A willingness to listen. The mother allowed her son to talk without interruption. She tried to understand her son without immediately offering solutions, becoming upset, or moralizing.

2. A willingness to accept the child's views and feelings. A way to establish a good relationship with your child is to attempt to understand and accept his or her views, opinions, and feelings. Such acceptance shows that you are listening; helps the child hear and understand his or her own feelings and thoughts; and communicates that it is acceptable to display one's feelings. At the same time, such acceptance does not necessarily mean that you agree with the child's ideas (e.g., "School is stupid."; "Nobody likes me."), but that you are trying to understand what he or she is saying. This process is the basis for future problem solving.

3. A willingness to make empathic responses. *Empathy* is a Greek word which literally means "suffering in". While empathizing, an individual attempts to identify with somebody else's thoughts, feelings, and emotions. In the current context, this type of response serves to acknowledge the child's feelings and demonstrates the parent's willingness to understand and accept.

Building and maintaining sound parent-child relationships is not easy. Yet, parents can improve less than satisfactory relationships by:

1. Practicing effective listening with their children;

2. Recognizing the existence and right of children's viewpoints and feelings; and

3. *Empathically* responding to children's thoughts and feelings.

Exercises for Improving Communication

The techniques for improving communication presented in this section may be new to you. The techniques may not come naturally—you will need to practice—and your child may not respond. With time and effort, however, you can improve your relationship with your children. Before trying out the techniques with your child, we recommend that you complete the following exercises.

Exercise 1: *Choose the best response.*

Child: (Upon entering the house after school): "If that stupid teacher calls, you can tell her I'm not ever going back!"

Parent: (a) "Sounds like you had a tough day."

(b) "What happened? Why is the teacher going to call me?"

(c) "This is not a good day for you to have screwed up in school—I've got my own problems today."

(d) "Wait until your father gets home and we will solve this thing—We will help you find a way to do better in school."

In this example the first response (a) was most appropriate. The parent sent the message that she was interested and willing to listen. In addition, she attempted to communicate that she was aware and accepting of her son's feelings.

Response (b) was accusatory. Hence, little or no productive interaction could be expected as a result.

Response (c) revealed parental disinterest and an unwillingness to listen. As with response (b) little productive conversation could be expected. Responses of this type routinely lead to resentment and anger.

Response (d) conveyed an interest in solving the problem, but not an understanding of the child's feelings and perceptions. Adequate solutions are unlikely to occur under such conditions.

Exercise 2: *Choose the best response.*

Parent: (At the dinner table): "What did you do today?"
Child: "Same as always—Nothing!—Nobody around here will play with me."
Parent: (a) "Maybe if you weren't such a bully kids would want to play with you."
 (b) "When I was a kid I had more friends than you could shake a stick at."
 (c) "Sounds kind of lonely."
 (d) "I'm going to call some parents after dinner—I think I know how to get some kids to play with you."

Response (c) is the preferred parental response. It communicates interest and an understanding of the child's feelings. It should open the door to further discussion and, eventually, solutions.

Response (a) is accusatory and will probably provoke a defensive explanation (e.g., "I only fight to protect myself.), anger or withdrawal.

Response (b) communicates disinterest. The parent is more interested in talking about his own childhood than in hearing about his son's perceptions and feelings.

Response (d) is a solution statement. Regardless of how well intended, this approach denies the child an opportunity to share his perceptions and feelings. While such a strategy might eventually be appropriate, it is incorrectly timed as an initial response.

Exercise 3: *Add your own response.*

Child: "I have all these chores to do. Wanda (sister) never has to do anything."
Parent: _____
_____
_____
_____

Your response should reflect the child's feelings and perceptions without displaying anger or resentment; disinterest; or a quick solution. Perhaps something like, "Sounds like household chores are getting you down."

How did you do? You should now be ready to try this technique with your child. Remember to be patient and give the technique time to work.

Summary

Parents and other family members play a prominent role in the growth and development of their children. They serve as referral agents and advocates; behavior managers; and communication sources. Adequately fulfilling all these roles is essential. Thus, parents must seek appropriate professional services; establish fair, yet firm rules; use management techniques to deal with specific problems; and communicate with their children. The degree of success with which these roles are fulfilled often influences the ability of children and youth to satisfactorily meet life's many demands.

What About the Future?

8

One question that cannot be adequately answered for *any* child focuses on what the future will bring. Since the late 1970s, more research has been published and more programs have been developed about the emotionally disturbed and behaviorally disordered than ever before. Nevertheless, even using the best treatment programs, it is impossible to make predictions about the future success of any child or adolescent.

With appropriate education/treatment, children and youth who are emotionally disturbed and/or behaviorally disordered may improve. Without such treatment or education, improvement is unlikely. Research has suggested that by ignoring the problems presented by these students, little progress is achieved. Specifically, the students' feelings and behaviors do not become more appropriate, and other students and teachers do not react to them more favorably as a result of exposure and familiarity.

Professionals must conduct long-term studies to allow better decisions regarding particular programs and their merit for individual students. It is the authors' belief that the educational and therapeutic climate for students with emotional disturbance and behavioral disorders has markedly improved. Such future studies will allow others to use some of the ideas and programs that are currently being practiced.

How long will it be before my child becomes "normal"?

The answer to this question will not come as a surprise to the reader. Some children show remarkable progress after they have been exposed to a special education and/or therapy program. They learn about themselves and acquire appropriate social skills needed to successfully coexist in the classroom, home, and community.

Other children, who "misbehave" because of immaturity, naturally outgrow their problem behaviors. However, there is no timetable. A student does not mystically "grow up." Children react differently to their environment. How and if students will react to new programs may depend upon their willingness (not necessarily ours!) to succeed, their ability, and their school program. Consider the following remarks from a special education elementary school teacher:

> Fred did not want to be placed in my special education classroom. He did not think that there was anything wrong with him, and there was "no way" that he was going into the "retarded room" (nobody in the room was mentally retarded). And, I wondered what the hell I was going to do with another student in an already crowded classroom.

> It's almost like you know the questions that parents are going to ask. They expect answers to questions that nobody knows how to answer. There isn't any guarantee that *anything* will work.

> It's funny. During my first year of teaching, I told parents that their children would be "cured" within a year or two. After all, I had just completed training at a university where I was taught what to do to teach these kids. I was confident that I could change them. I know now that not every child can be helped by me. I know now that, for many students, change is an extremely long and difficult, and maybe impossible task. How do I give a parent this information?

> I have been teaching for 12 years and I have seen so many success stories. Children who supposedly were lost souls are now gainfully employed. I seriously doubt that they would have made it without this school program. Failures? You bet! But every success has

immeasurable worth, because these were the children that everyone gave up on.

The teacher quoted above gives a realistic appraisal of current conditions and hopes for students in the schools. While these comments are not optimistic, they do give hope to those who continue to strive for an appropriate education. Interestingly, this teacher's remarks do not differ much from those of others who work and live with children who have emotional and behavioral disorders. Harsh realities and hope permeate their statements.

I see so many children that enter school with the odds against them. Some are shy and withdrawn, others are totally out of control. I believe that the earlier I can begin working with the classroom teacher, and, ideally, the parents, the more progress can be made. Unfortunately, a lot of my time is spent on paperwork and not enough on "kidwork." But, there are times when everything falls into place and we have a child who is going to "make it." (school psychologist)

My job is working in the home with children and their families. Many students have their problems because of family problems. When families are cooperative and see me as being helpful, major positive changes occur. Other families see me as a threat to them and become quite defensive. They are too busy, or unwilling, or, in many cases, going through major personal changes themselves to concentrate on working together. While I sometimes get quite upset that they won't work, I understand their situations. Further, the successes with these so-called helpless cases make my job extremely rewarding. (school social worker)

I used to be very pushy with my son's teachers. I believed that the only way he was going to get a fair shake from his teachers was with my help. What I got from them was a lot of resistance that made me angrier. One teacher, however, took the time to listen. When she listened, I began to listen and we began to cooperate with each other. I have found that more of my concerns are now being attended to, and that I have a more positive relationship with the school, *which is resulting in a better education for my son!* My son recently said to me that he likes school more now because I seem to be happy with it. Needless to say, that really blew my mind! (parent)

Some children may never be "normal." That is, they will continue to behave in a manner that may require assistance from others. The greatest hurdle facing parents, children, and teachers is to accept that for these children, emotional disturbance is as much a handicap as being paraplegic. However, many emotionally disturbed/behaviorally disordered students can achieve happy and meaningful lives.

Does that mean that people with behavioral and emotional handicaps will be more accepted in the future?

This is a difficult question to answer. While society has progressed in the way it treats emotionally handicapped individuals, it has *generally* kept these individuals isolated. People who disturb others are not usually accepted. People whose behaviors are very different from others, usually call attention to themselves and are perceived in a negative fashion. Unlike learning disabilities and, to some degree, mild mental retardation, emotional and behavioral handicaps are more overt or obvious, and, consequently, more troubling to others.

Society must decide the direction it wants to take with respect to emotionally and behaviorally disordered individuals. Research to help determine "what works" is needed. Also, research must help prevent and treat biophysical causes of emotional disturbance. In addition, important questions such as the following must be addressed:

Can the public develop a more tolerant position about the emotionally disturbed and behaviorally disordered?

Will education and public awareness help this process?

Do people understand that emotional disturbance is a handicap? That is, it is similar to a physical handicap.

Are federal, state, and local authorities willing to provide increased financial assistance for training, intervention, and research?

Will my child finish school?

This depends upon you, your child, and the school. Not all students with emotional and behavioral problems finish school. By the time Bobby reaches adolescence, you may be tired of fighting for his educational rights. He may be tired of trying to "fit in." And his teachers may be tired of fighting the system. Consider the following teacher's report:

> They [the emotionally disturbed or behaviorally disordered] arrive, occasionally within a few hours of placement, eyes scared, confused, defiant, resigned. Eventually, most begin to relax, communicate, and to work with you, toward, hopefully, more progressively than regressively, a resolution, or, at least a compromise. Some fail. Every child and situation is unique. What happens to these unreachables? Some drop out of school, become (juvenile) delinquents, return to delinquency, or, simply "survive." Some come back to visit with an "I wish I had . . .", or, "If only . . .", or, "It's not like I thought . . .". They just know that it would be different if they could "do it again."

> Attempts to advise their former fellow classmates fall upon deaf ears (no longer a peer, no longer trusted?). They didn't make it! Why should I listen?

> Some might return to night school, some might find jobs, maybe not the ones that they were sure they would get, but, at least, something. Others return to their families, or, to friends until their "welcome" wears thin. Where do they turn? Are they future "Social Services" candidates?

> Yet, there are others who *do* want to do something with their lives! They have goals! They are not precisely sure of the exactness of the goals, but they believe that they need an education to achieve anything. They work hard to read. They want desperately to be like everybody else.

If Bobby becomes frustrated and disgusted with school, he may stop going to classes. If Bobby gets suspended enough times, he might find himself pushed out of school. Many teachers and schools do not try to keep disturbing students in class. Therefore they may not look for Bobby when he misses classes, or the school may suspend him from classes for missing classes (!?!).

Another possibility is that Bobby may be placed in a residential treatment program or institution because of his inability to conform to the behavioral expectations of the school, or because of continuous problems with the law.

Therefore, it is extremely important that the school, parent(s), and Bobby work closely together to insure not only that Bobby finishes school, but that he is adequately prepared to enter adulthood.

Is Fred going to be brainwashed or become a "robot"?

This question stems from a very common misconception about special education treatment, especially when it involves the use of behavior modification. Fred will be taught new ways to react to events that were formerly very upsetting to him. Hopefully, as a result, he will be "different", that is, he will not react or feel so intensely negative as he does now. It will not make him a "robot." It will not make him a "stranger." Instead, treatment will decrease the intensity of the feelings and behaviors that have prevented Fred from functioning adequately in school.

What guarantees do I have that my child will succeed?

None. Each child reacts differently to intervention and treatment. If change does occur, factors such as your child's ability and willingness to change must be considered. Many older students seem to have the attitude that "There's nothing wrong with me. These guys and you are crazy," making change more difficult to achieve. Younger children are often more willing to take the risks needed to change.

The needs of emotionally disturbed children and youth are still not being met satisfactorily in all school districts. While more students are being identified as having emotional disturbances and behavioral disorders and the number of programs have increased, the success of such trends has not been determined. Most schools have the best interests of the student in mind; however, you must have a clear understanding of their intentions, and how they hope to achieve those intentions.

Is Fred going to get married and have children?

Perhaps. It depends on the severity of Fred's problems. While some emotionally disturbed and behaviorally disordered youth get married, others live with their parents, in group homes, or in institutions. Many live at home with their parents because of the scarcity of appropriate housing. If they get a job, they may find a roommate to share expenses and responsibilities. Group homes for the mildly handicapped are still rare, and often maintain long waiting lists.

Will I be responsible for my son when he reaches adulthood?

You need not be legally responsible. If supervision is still needed, legal guardianship can be attained after your child reaches the age of 21 if you so desire. Of course, it is necessary to contemplate many factors before you arrive at this decision. Two important issues to consider are:

1. The severity of your child's disability. Does he exhibit behaviors that can be dangerous to himself or others?
2. Your age(s). How will guardianship and any transition to a different type of custodianship affect the need for future care?

What type of job will my daughter get?

Without job training, many emotionally disturbed or behaviorally disordered students will be unable to obtain and maintain jobs.

It is important to remember that a common reason for dismissal from jobs is *not* the employee's inability to demonstrate specific skills, but the inability to function in harmony with others.

Most school systems have vocational programs for students with special needs. With cooperation from the schools, your child should have an Individualized Education Program that includes a meaningful occupational/vocational training component. Hopefully, such a plan will include information about employment opportunities in your community.

Will future children we may have also be emotionally handicapped?

Unless your child's handicap is attributed to heredity, that is, a genetic predisposition to emotional illness, there is little to indicate that any future children you may have will be similarly affected. Further, since any genetic link is rare, it should not be the sole factor in your decision regarding having more children. While genetics (e.g., many cases of mental illness in the family) may contribute to the child's chances of having emotional problems, a strong and caring family equally contributes to a child's emotional health.

Will my child's children be emotionally handicapped?

Again, research has pointed to a (weak) link between heredity and mental illness. The type of emotional problems your child exhibits is significant here. The vast majority of those identified and treated for emotional and/or behavioral problems *do not* have problems because of heredity.

Raising a family is an extremely demanding process, even under ideal conditions. Parents who cannot manage their intense feelings and/or behaviors may have difficulty raising emotionally healthy children.

Summary

The purpose of this book is to give those who live and work with children and youth who have emotional and behavioral problems, a foundation from which to begin to understand the complexities that exist in the educational and therapeutic process. We have tried to address issues about the school, the home, the community, and the difficulties inherent in dealing with each, sometimes juggling them, so that children can successfully complete school and progress into adulthood.

Parents and others who work with emotionally disturbed and behaviorally disordered students must be made aware of what these children can be taught, and, more importantly, what kind of goals they can be expected to achieve.

Many dedicated teachers and support staff who work with emotionally disturbed and behaviorally disordered youth are trying to help them cope with their handicap. For every success there will probably be a failure. Some students with emotional disturbances and behavioral disorders may attend college, others may land in jail. Some will lead fruitful social lives, others may be alone.

There are opportunities for those who have the ability and help to take advantage of them. There is a hope for a full and productive life for those who can learn to handle their problems and develop the skills necessary to function in an ever-changing and demanding society.

There is a direct relationship between the time and effort spent on ensuring a student's rights to an appropriate education and his or her success. Hopefully, this book will aid this process.

Glossary of Terms

Achievement test: A test designed to measure a person's knowledge and understanding in a particular area (e.g., math, reading).

Acute: A term used to describe the rapid onset of symptoms.

Adaptive behavior: A term used to describe the degree to which persons are able to be self-sufficient and meet social responsibility standards for their age and cultural group.

Advocacy: A term used to describe the support or representation of another person or group's interests.

Affect: Relating to emotions or feelings.

Affective disorder: Any one of a number of problems of emotion or feelings, including depression.

Aggressive behavior: Assaultive action or other response which interferes with the rights of others.

Anorexia nervosa: An eating disorder characterized by a pathological loss of appetite.

Antidepressant drugs: Medications designed to alleviate depression and related emotional problems.

Antisocial personality: A personality disturbance characterized by a general lack of socialization and behaviors that repeatedly clash with societal standards. Persons with this disorder may also be referred to as *sociopathic*.

Anxiety: A term used to describe emotional tension and confusion.

Anxiety disorder: A disorder characterized by anxiety, anxious overconcern, and somatic complaints.

Aphasia: A disorder characterized by loss or impairment of language production and/or comprehension. Aphasia results from brain injury or disease.

Attention deficit disorder: A term used to describe children with attention and impulse control problems. In the past, this condition has been referred to as *hyperkinetic* syndrome and *hyperactivity*.

Audiologists: Professionals whose role is to evaluate and make recommendations regarding children's hearing deficits.

Autism: A communication and behavioral disorder which begins in early childhood. Children with autism are characterized by speech and language problems, developmental delays, social deficits, and behavioral disorders.

Baseline: A behavior modification term for the frequency, rate, or duration of a behavior prior to intervention.

Behavioral disorder: A term used to describe children and youth whose behavior is chronically so inappropriate as to interfere with educational, family, and community adjustment. The terms *emotional disturbance, emotional impairment, social maladjustment, emotionally handicapped,* and *conduct disordered* are also used to describe this disorder.

Behaviorally impaired: See *behavioral disorder.*

Behavior modification: A treatment and educational approach wherein consequences are used to create planned behavior changes. *Applied behavior analysis, operant conditioning, behavior therapy,* and *behavioral strategy* are also used to describe this strategy.

Behavior rating scale: A test, usually completed by parents and teachers, describing the frequency and extent of persons' social and interpersonal behavior patterns.

Biochemical imbalance: Internal chemical deficiencies or imbalances thought to cause disturbed behavior or feelings.

Brain damage: Also known as *neurological impairment* and *minimal brain damage,* this term refers to any one of a number of conditions resulting from damage or malformation of the brain and/or spinal cord.

Bulimia: This condition, also known as *polyphagia*, refers to pathological overeating.

Catharsis: A psychotherapeutic term referring to the release to consciousness of repressed information, usually through a discussion process.

Central nervous system (CNS) stimulant drugs: These drugs are designed to reduce attention deficit problems, including hyperactivity, by stimulating the central nervous system. Common CNS stimulant medications include Ritalin and Cylert.

Character disorder: A severe personality disorder characterized by insensitivity and socially unacceptable patterns.

Childhood asthma: A disease of childhood wherein attacks of breathing, caused by bronchial constriction, are the primary characteristics.

Chromosome: The part of the cell which carries hereditary information.

Chronic: A term used to describe a condition of long duration.

Cognitive: A term referring to any one of a number of mental processes, including memory.

Cognitive behavior therapy: A treatment approach based on a combination of psychotherapy and behavior modification.

Compulsion: An urge or thought to perform an unwanted act.

Conduct disorder: A term used to describe behavior which interferes with the rights of others and/or societal norms as well as a person's maximal learning and social development.

Conflict: A general term used to describe a mental struggle arising from opposing drives or needs.

Congenital: A term used to describe a condition or characteristic present at birth.

Consequences: A behavior modification term used to describe the use of positive reinforcers and punishers to change behavior.

Constitutional: This term refers to a person's physical structure and body build.

Consultant model: A special education support service wherein a student's regular class teachers receive consultation from another professional.

Crisis intervention: An emergency service or procedure used to meet urgent needs or circumstances.

Cultural deprivation: A term used to describe problems associated with low socioeconomic conditions, limited stimulation, and familial disorganization.

Day school: A daytime educational facility designed exclusively for handicapped students.

Defense mechanism: An unconscious process used by all persons to protect them from anxiety and emotional conflict. Common defense mechanisms include projection, rationalization, and repression.

Delayed speech: A term used to describe the development of speech or language which is slower than the norm.

Delusion: A false belief, including delusions of persecution and identity.

Depression: A pathological sadness or melancholy demeanor.

Detention facility: A correctional facility for convicted or alleged juvenile offenders or other juveniles requiring restricted quarters.

Developmental disability: A broad term referring to any one of a number of severe and chronic disabilities which set in prior to adulthood. The term includes mental retardation, cerebral palsy, and autism.

Developmental history: A history or record of a person's significant developmental events, including milestones, illnesses, etc.

Diagnostic and Statistical Manual of Mental Disorders: DSM-111–Revised is a manual which lists and defines psychiatric conditions recognized by the American Psychiatric Association.

Drive: A term used to describe a basic urge, instinct, or motivation.

Due process: A component of the Education for All Handicapped Children Act, which provides rights and privileges to handicapped pupils and their parents, including the right to a hearing to arbitrate differences with school systems.

Duration: A term used to describe the length of time a problem is present.

Dyslexia: An impairment of reading ability.

Echolalia: A speech condition characterized by repetition of others' words or sounds. Echolalia is a common characteristic of children with autism and certain other severe emotional disturbances.

Education for All Handicapped Children Act: A federal law which protects the rights of handicapped children and youth.

Educationally handicapped: A general term used to describe children and youth who experience behavior and learning problems.

Ego: A psychoanalytic term used to refer to the conscious reality part of the personality. According to Freud, the ego serves as an arbitrator between one's inner needs (see id) and external reality.

Elective mutism: Voluntary refusal to talk.

Emotional disturbance: A term used to describe behavior and feelings which interfere with day-to-day functioning. The term is often used interchangeably with *behavior disorder, conduct disorder, emotional handicap, social maladjustment,* and *mental illness.*

Emotionally handicapped: See *emotional disturbance* or *behavioral disorder.*

Encopresis: Lack of bowel control not associated with physical defect or disease.

Enuresis: Involuntary discharge of urine, often occurring during sleep.

Extinction: A behavior modification term used to describe the withdrawal of reinforcement (usually attention) as a means of reducing the occurrence of a problem behavior. The term "planned ignoring" is also used to describe extinction.

Family counseling: See *family therapy.*

Family therapy: A term used to describe the simultaneous psychotherapeutic treatment of more than one member of a family. Thus, the family of a child with behavioral problems may be seen together.

Fixation: A psychoanalytic theory term referring to arrest of psychosexual maturation. For example, a child may be arrested in the anal phase of development.

Function disorder: A disorder of elimination or eating.

Genetic: Relating to heredity, or characteristics transmitted from parents to children.

Hard neurological sign: This term refers to specific and identifiable neurological damage responsible for a particular problem.

Halfway house: A term used to describe a residence for persons needing specialized treatment and attention but who are able to function without full hospitalization or institutionalization.

Hallucination: A memory image mistaken for reality. Thus, persons may hear or see nonexistent sounds or objects.

Homebound instruction: A special education delivery alternative whereby students receive instruction at home by a special education teacher.

Hyperactivity: Behavior characterized by excessive activity and/or movement.

Id: A psychoanalytic term used to refer to that part of the personality which contains unconscious instincts and needs.

Identity crisis: A term used to describe difficulty in accepting or adopting a person's role and self-perception to what is expected by society.

Incidence: The extent or frequency of a disorder.

Individualized Education Program (IEP): A component of The Education for All Handicapped Children's Act (EHA) requiring that each handicapped student has an individually prepared instructional and treatment plan. Each IEP is prepared by a team, including the parent.

Individualized Implementation Plan (IIP): The component of the Individualized Education Program (IEP) which identifies goals, objectives, and intervention strategies.

Insight: A term commonly used in psychotherapy to refer to the degree to which a person understands the origin and nature of his problems.

Intensity: A term used to describe the severity or degree of a person's problems.

Juvenile delinquency: A term used to describe youngsters who have committed legal and social offenses.

Learning disability: A disorder characterized by deficits of achievement and/or language.

Least restrictive environment: A component of the Education for All Handicapped Children Act of 1975 whereby children and youth are to be served in maximally normalized settings. Thus, emotionally disturbed children will only be served in residential and other restrictive settings when their needs cannot appropriately be met in less restrictive settings.

Libido: A psychoanalytic term used to describe psychic energy.

Life space interview: A psychoeducational procedure designed to assist children in understanding and changing their behavior.

Mainstreaming: The education of handicapped students within regular school classes, as opposed to placement of handicapped pupils in segregated settings.

Major tranquilizers: Tranquilizer drugs designed to reduce problems associated with severe emotional and behavioral disturbances. These medications are also known as *phenothiazines.*

Mental health clinic: A facility designed to provide mental health services.

Minimal brain damage: See *brain damage.*

Multidisciplinary team: An assessment team composed of professionals representing a variety of disciplines.

Neologism: A coined word. Such words are relatively common in persons with schizophrenia.

Neonatal: Pertaining to the first month following birth.

Nondiscriminatory assessment: Use of educational and psychological measures that are not prejudicial, either because of a child's handicap, ethnicity, culture, or language.

Obesity: Pathological body weight.

Obsessive-compulsive: A personality disorder characterized by recurrent obsessions and compulsions. Obsessions are recurrent unwanted ideas, thoughts, or urges while compulsions are repetitive actions a person feels compelled to engage in (e.g., touching every fifth crack on a sidewalk).

Occupational therapist: Professional whose role is to diagnose and treat children's daily living and self-help problems.

Oedipus complex: A psychoanalytic term characterized by a child's interest and attachment to the parent of the opposite sex and his or her envy and competitive feelings toward the parent of the same sex.

Overcorrection: Behavior modification technique used to decrease unacceptable behavior. The restitution part of overcorrection requires that children clean up or restore a situation they disturb, while positive practice, the second part of overcorrection, involves having children practice appropriate alternatives to unacceptable behavior (e.g., stacking blocks for throwing).

Paranoia: A term used to describe persons who are overly suspicious, including those with delusions of persecution.

Passive-aggressive: A term used to describe persons who display aggression in passive ways. This disorder is exemplified by a child who is intentionally inefficient in completing household chores.

Pattern: A description of the specific time, place, and/or circumstances associated with a child's problems.

Perceptual-motor: This term is used to describe various motor activities that interact with perception, including visual and auditory activities.

Perseveration: A term used to describe a pathological persistence of an idea or action.

Personality disorder: A group of mental disorders characterized by deeply ingrained and chronic patterns of maladaptive behavior.

Phobia: A term used to describe a persistent and irrational fear (e.g., fear of dogs).

Physical therapist: Professional whose role is to diagnose and treat physical ability and muscle control problems.

Pica: A term used to describe a craving for unnatural foods (e.g., children who eat dirt).

Play therapy: A psychotherapy approach wherein children are allowed to express their feelings and emotions through play activities and toys.

Pleasure principle: The psychoanalytic concept that man purportedly has an instinct to avoid discomfort and strive for pleasure.

Precipitating: Specific incidents or conditions which may trigger a problem or condition.

Predisposing: Inherited potential for certain problems or conditions.

Prognosis: A prediction of future outcome of a condition (e.g., the probability that a child with an emotional problem will be independent and productive as an adult).

Projection: A defense mechanism characterized by a person projecting onto others unacceptable emotions and feelings.

Projective method: An unstructured personality assessment procedure whereby persons are asked to respond to an ambiguous stimulus (e.g., ink blot), thereby giving personality information to an examiner. Projective methods include the *Rorschach* test and sentence-completion tests.

Psychiatrist: Physician whose role is to diagnose and apply psychotherapeutic procedures with children and youth having emotional and behavioral problems.

Psychoanalysis: A theory human development and behavior and a specific form of psychotherapy based on the teachings of Sigmund Freud. In psychoanalysis treatment, persons are aided in understanding unconscious conflicts and issues.

Psychodynamic: A theory of human behavior wherein unconscious and conscious drives and needs are considered to be primary components.

Psychoeducational: The adaptation of psychoanalytic and psychotherapeutic principles for educational use.

Psychologist: Professional whose role is to use tests, interviews, and observation techniques to make judgments about cognitive, academic, personality, and perceptual strengths and weaknesses. Psychologists are also frequently involved in treating and counseling behaviorally disordered children and adolescents.

Psychomotor: A term used to refer to sensory and perceptual factors as they relate to motor skills.

Psychosexual development: A term of human development from psychoanalytic theory according to which a child's development and personality are influenced by developmental experiences. Developmental stages include oral phase, anal phase, phallic phase, latency period, and genital phase.

Psychosis: A broad classification of severe emotional disturbances signifying that a person's ability to function is significantly impaired.

Psychosomatic: A term used to describe physical disorders associated with emotional problems.

Psychotherapy: Any one of a number of psychiatric or psychological counseling and treatment methods based on verbal and/or nonverbal communication.

Psychotropic medication: Prescription drugs whose purpose is to influence behavior, mood, and thought processes.

Punisher: A behavior modification term used to describe a consequence which decreases the probability of the behavior it follows. The term "negative consequence" is also used to describe a punisher.

Rational-emotive therapy: A form of cognitive behavior therapy. Also referred to as *rational-emotive therapy, rational-behavioral therapy, rational-emotive education,* and *reality therapy,* this approach involves training children to correct their inaccurate perceptions.

Rationalization: A defense mechanism wherein a person attempts to justify or provide a socially acceptable explanation for a given behavior.

Reality principle: A psychoanalytic theory notion that the pleasure principle (see *pleasure principle*) is modified by the demands and conditions of the real world.

Regular classroom: A term used to describe non-special education school programs.

Reinforcer: A behavior modification term used to describe a consequence that increases the probability of the behavior it follows. Common reinforcers are *contingent activities* and *social consequences* (e.g., smiles, hugs).

Repression: A defense mechanism whereby unacceptable or unpleasant thoughts are kept from consciousness.

Residential program: A facility wherein children and youth are provided 24-hour care. Such programs typically serve the needs of seriously disturbed children and adolescents and those requiring crisis services.

Resource room: A term for a special education model where teachers provide specialized instruction to students for part of the school day. Resource room teachers may also provide consultation services to regular classroom teachers.

Response cost: A behavior modification term used to describe the systematic removal of rewards for unacceptable behavior.

Schizoid disorder: A term used to describe a disorder whose primary characteristic is the inability to form meaningful social relationships.

Schizophrenia: Any one of several psychotic conditions characterized by disturbances of thought, mood, and behavior.

School phobia: A fear of school, usually manifesting itself in school avoidance.

Screening: A brief diagnostic procedure designed to identify children and youth requiring detailed evaluation.

Self-contained special class: A special class where students are taught by the same teacher(s) throughout the day.

Self-mutilation: A term used to describe behavior intended to inflict self-harm or abuse.

Self-stimulation: A term used to describe purposeless, repetitive behaviors, including rocking, hand-waving, etc. Such responses are common among autistic-like children.

Sedative medications: Drugs designed to reduce anxiety and otherwise control less extreme emotional problems.

Separation anxiety: Fear and anxiety associated with separation from a significant person (e.g., parent) or familiar surroundings.

Sheltered workshop: A work facility for handicapped persons who are unable to function in regular work settings. Such settings are usually reserved for persons with severe emotional problems and severe developmental disabilities.

Social maladjustment: A term used to describe persons who refuse to abide by rules and societal standards. The term is frequently used interchangeably with *emotional disturbance* and *social maladjustment*.

Social worker: Professional involved in gathering social history, diagnostic information, and coordinating treatment and educational services. Social workers may also be involved in counseling and psychotherapy.

Socialized delinquent: A term used to describe children or youth who engage in delinquent activities, usually in group settings or with peers.

Soft neurological sign: This term is used to describe mild, alleged (unidentifiable) damage assumed to cause specific problems or characteristics.

Somatic: Relating to the body.

Special educator: Educator specifically trained to diagnose and teach students having emotional and behavioral problems (or other exceptionalities). A special educator may work directly with students or consult with other teachers.

Speech pathologist: Professional whose role is to diagnose and treat communication impairments.

Standardization group: A term used to refer to a group of persons against whom an individual is compared in diagnostic testing. For example, in standardized intelligence testing, children are compared with similar groups of children on various tasks.

Superego: A psychoanalytic term used to describe the part of the personality that is concerned with conscience and socially acceptable pursuits.

Substance abuse: Pathological use of alcohol, medications, narcotics, or other potentially harmful substances.

Thought disorder: Pathological thoughts, beliefs, or ideas.

Time-out: A behavior modification technique involving the removal of a child from reinforcement for unacceptable behavior. For example, a child may be made to sit quietly in a corner for 3 minutes whenever he tantrums.

Ulcerative colitis: A disease characterized by ulceration of the colon and rectum.

Unconscious motivation: A term frequently used in psychoanalytic theory to refer to thoughts and needs unavailable to conscious awareness.

Withdrawal: A term used to describe a significant retreat from people or reality.

Resources

In many states local, state, and regional organizations, both parent and professional, serve as resources to parents. Two resources to contact include your state Board of Education, Office of Special Education, and your state chapter of the Council for Children with Behavioral Disorders, a division of the Council for Exceptional Children. To locate contact persons in the Council for Children with Behavioral Disorders, write:

Council for Children with Behavioral Disorders
Council for Exceptional Children
1920 Association Drive
Reston, VA 22091-1589

Other organizations that may be of service:

American Association of Psychiatric Clinics for Children
250 W. Fifty-Seventh Street
New York, NY 10019

American Personnel and Guidance Association
5203 Leesburg Pike
Falls Church, VA 22041

American Printing House for the Blind
1839 Frankfort Avenue
Louisville, KY 40206

American Psychological Association
1200 17th Street, NW
Washington, DC 20036

Association for Children and Adults with Learning Disabilities
4156 Library Road
Pittsburgh, PA 15234

Association for Persons with Severe Handicaps
7010 Roosevelt Way NE
Seattle, WA 98115

Association for Retarded Citizens of the United States
2501 Avenue J
Arlington, TX 76006

Autism Society of America
1234 Massachusetts Avenue NW
Suite 1017
Washington, DC 20005

Center for Innovation in Teaching the Handicapped
Indiana University
2805 East Tenth St.
Bloomington, IN 47405

Child Welfare League of America
67 Irving Place
New York, NY 10003

Closer Look—National Information Center for the Handicapped
1201 16th Street, NW
Washington, DC 20036

Co-Ordinating Council for Handicapped Children
407 South Dearborn, Room 400
Chicago, IL 60605

Council for Learning Disabilities
P.O. Box 40303
Overland Park, KS 66204

Foundation for Children with Learning Disabilities
99 Park Avenue
New York, NY 10016

March of Dimes
1275 Mamaroneck Avenue
White Plains, NY 10605

National Association for the Education of Young Children
1834 Connecticut Avenue, NW
Washington, DC 20009

National Association of Private Schools for Exceptional Children
7700 Miller Road
Miami, FL 33155

National Association of Protection and Advocacy Systems
300 I Street NE
Suite 212
Washington, DC 20002

National Center for the Prevention and Treatment of Child
   Abuse and Neglect
1205 Oneida Street
Denver, CO 80220

National Education Association
1201 Sixteenth Street, NW
Washington, DC 20036

National Easter Seal Society
2023 West Ogden Avenue
Chicago, IL 60612

National Information Center for Children and Youth
   with Handicaps
P.O. Box 1492
Washington, D.C. 20016